THE BIG BOOK OF
HOW THINGS WORK

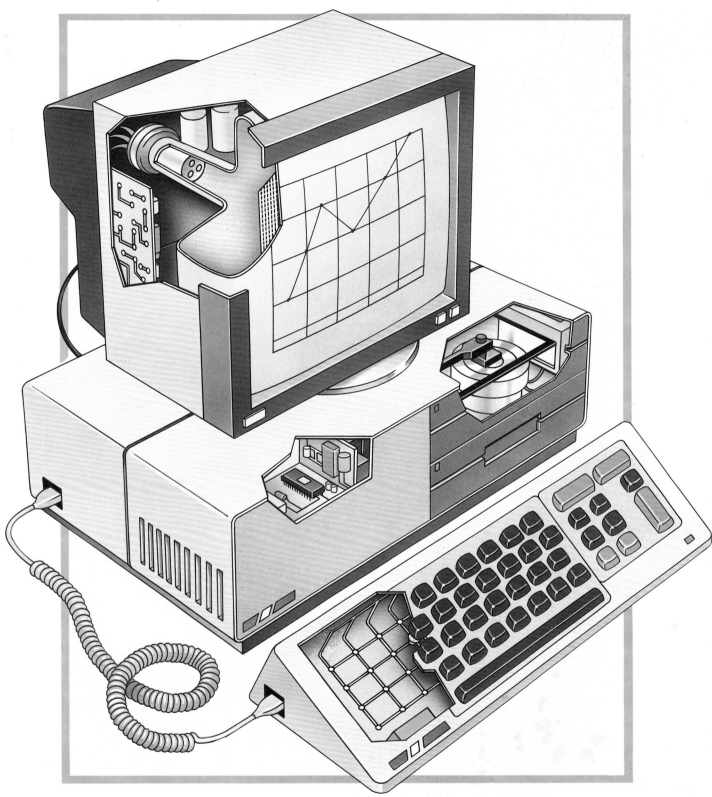

PETER LAFFERTY

GALLERY BOOKS
An Imprint of W. H. Smith Publishers Inc.
112 Madison Avenue
New York City 10016

First published in the United States in 1990 by Gallery books,
an imprint of W.H. Smith Publishers, Inc.,
112 Madison Avenue, New York 10016

By arrangement with The Octopus Publishing Group Limited,
Michelin House, 81 Fulham Road, London SW3 6RB

ISBN 0 8317 0859 X

Printed in Great Britain by BPCC Paulton Books Ltd.

Gallery Books are available for bulk purchase for sales promotions and
premium use. For details write or telephone the Manager of Special
Sales, W.H. Smith Publishers, Inc., 112 Madison Avenue, New York,
New York 10016. (212) 532–6600

CONTENTS

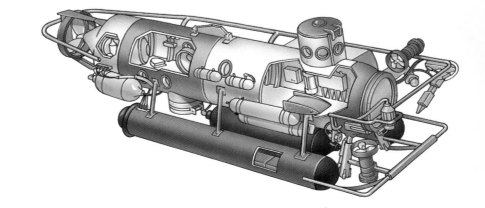

ELECTRICITY SUPPLY

Electricity is usually produced in power stations far away from the cities, factories, and homes that use the power. The electricity is sent to the users along large cables, called transmission lines.

In some power stations, coal or oil is burned to heat water and make steam. In a nuclear power station, water is heated by nuclear fuel to make steam (see pages 6–7). The steam produced flows over the windmill-like blades of a turbine, making the turbine turn swiftly. The steam is often sent through several turbines in turn, until all its heat energy is extracted.

The rotating turbines turn the generators. These consist of coils of wire which are rotated near an electromagnet. They produce alternating current (AC) electricity (see pages 10–11). The electricity produced is then sent to a device called a transformer.

A transformer can change the voltage, or electrical pressure, of an alternating electrical current. Some transformers, known as "step-up" transformers, can increase the voltage of an electric current. Other transformers, called "step-down" transformers, can reduce the voltage of a current.

Below: In the power station boiler, water is heated to become steam. The steam passes through the turbines, making the generator turn. The steam then goes to the cooling tower to be condensed back into water and reused. The transformer changes the electricity produced by the generator from about 11,000 volts to over 400,000 volts.

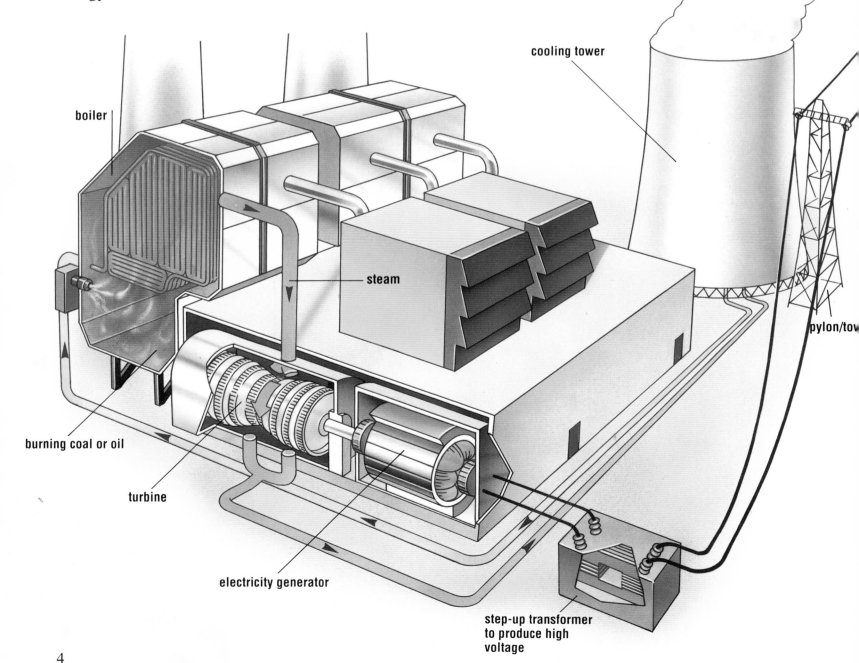

boiler

cooling tower

steam

burning coal or oil

turbine

electricity generator

pylon/tow

step-up transformer to produce high voltage

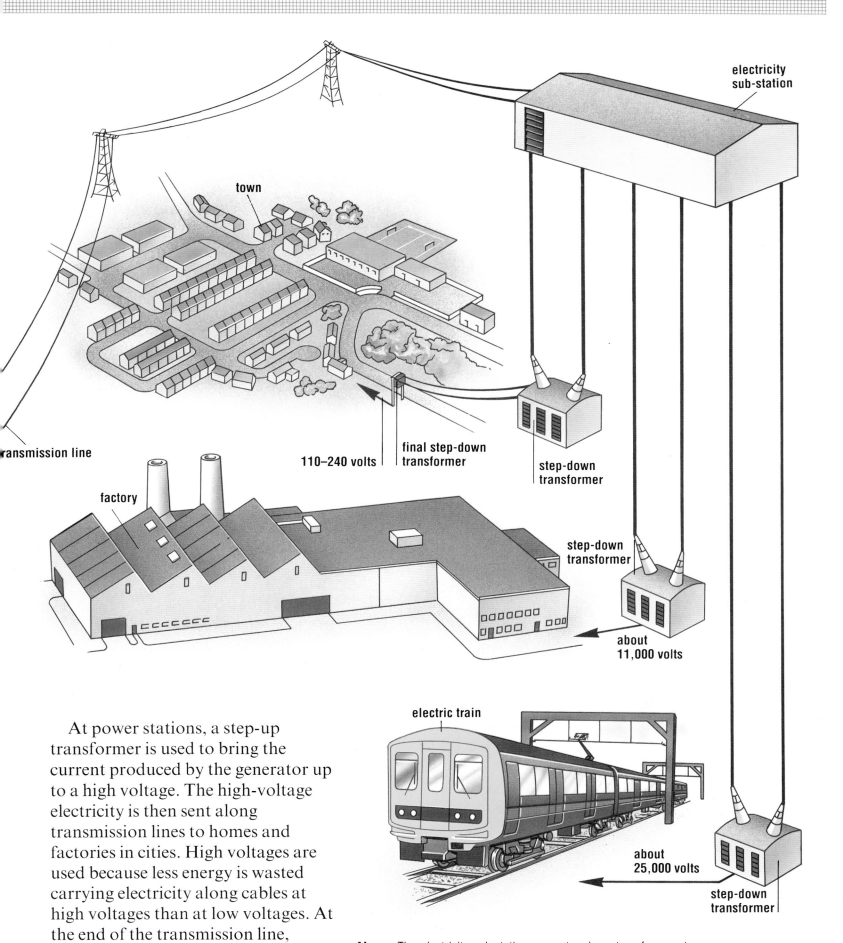

electricity
sub-station

town

transmission line

110–240 volts

final step-down
transformer

step-down
transformer

factory

step-down
transformer

about
11,000 volts

electric train

about
25,000 volts

step-down
transformer

At power stations, a step-up transformer is used to bring the current produced by the generator up to a high voltage. The high-voltage electricity is then sent along transmission lines to homes and factories in cities. High voltages are used because less energy is wasted carrying electricity along cables at high voltages than at low voltages. At the end of the transmission line, another transformer is used to reduce the voltage to a low level so that it can be safely used in homes and factories.

Above: The electricity sub-station uses step-down transformers to reduce the high voltage power from the transmission line to about 130,000 volts. The voltage is reduced even further by other transformers before it enters homes and factories.

THE NUCLEAR POWER STATION

reactor vessel

containment vessel

fuel rods

Right: Pressurized water reactors are the most common type of reactor worldwide. In them, water at high pressure heats up as it flows through the reactor vessel. The water then flows through the steam generator where it is turned into steam. The steam is piped to the turbines which turn the electricity generators.

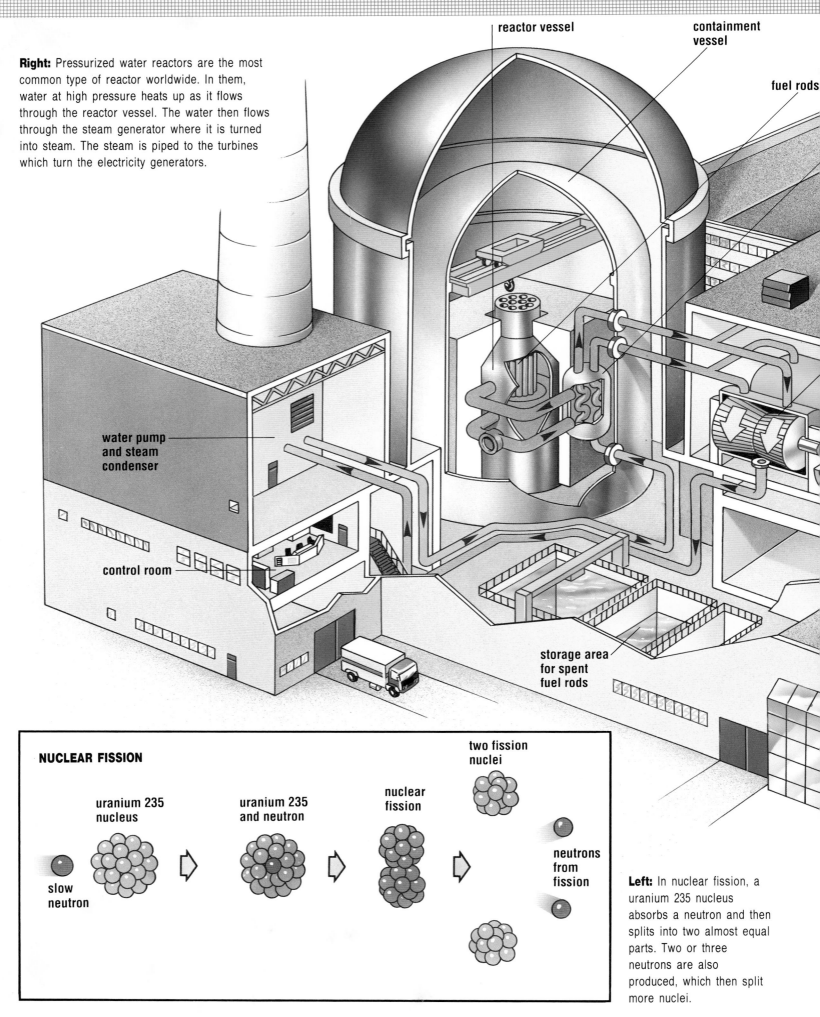

water pump and steam condenser

control room

storage area for spent fuel rods

NUCLEAR FISSION

two fission nuclei

uranium 235 nucleus

uranium 235 and neutron

nuclear fission

slow neutron

neutrons from fission

Left: In nuclear fission, a uranium 235 nucleus absorbs a neutron and then splits into two almost equal parts. Two or three neutrons are also produced, which then split more nuclei.

6

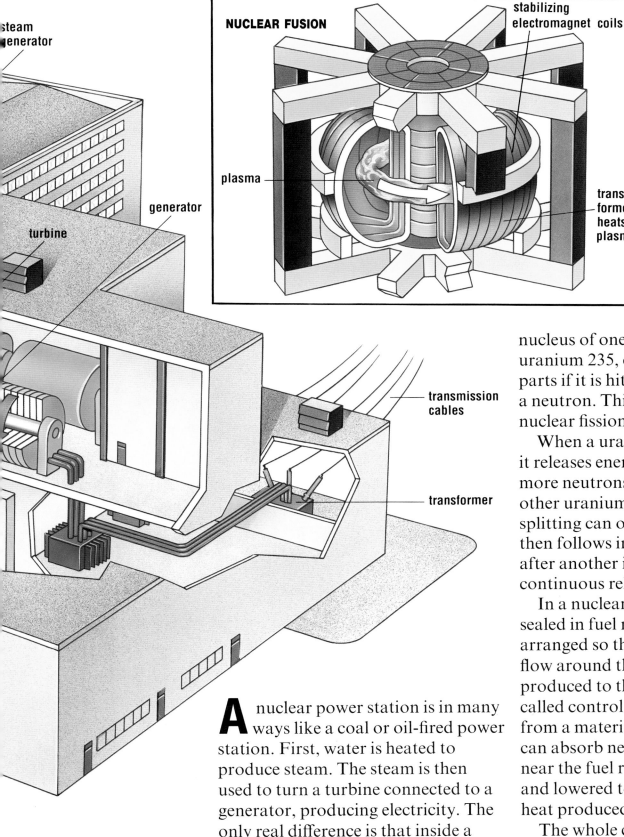

NUCLEAR FUSION

stabilizing
electromagnet coils

plasma

trans-
former
heats
plasma

steam
generator

generator

turbine

transmission
cables

transformer

Left: Scientists are trying to produce power by using the process that powers the Sun and stars: nuclear fusion. In fusion, nuclei of hydrogen join together to make helium nuclei, at the same time releasing energy. The hydrogen nuclei have to be heated to 100 million °C before this can happen. The experimental machines built to produce these enormous temperatures are called fusion reactors. They use magnetism to hold the hot gas, plasma, in place.

A nuclear power station is in many ways like a coal or oil-fired power station. First, water is heated to produce steam. The steam is then used to turn a turbine connected to a generator, producing electricity. The only real difference is that inside a nuclear station, uranium atoms are split apart to produce heat.

Atoms are the very small particles of which all materials consist. At the center of each one is a small, dense ball of matter called a nucleus. The nucleus of one type of uranium, called uranium 235, can be broken into parts if it is hit by a tiny particle called a neutron. This process is called nuclear fission.

When a uranium 235 nucleus splits, it releases energy and two or three more neutrons. If these neutrons hit other uranium atoms, further splitting can occur. A chain reaction then follows in which one nucleus after another is split, causing a continuous release of power.

In a nuclear reactor, uranium 235 is sealed in fuel rods. The rods are arranged so that a liquid or gas can flow around them to carry the heat produced to the boiler. Other rods called control rods, which are made from a material such as boron which can absorb neutrons, are arranged near the fuel rods. They can be raised and lowered to control the amount of heat produced by the fuel rods.

The whole collection of fuel and control rods is embedded in a material known as a moderator. This can be graphite or water. Its function is to slow down the neutrons produced. This makes the energy production process more efficient.

WATER SUPPLY

Right: Water is pumped from the reservoir to the sedimentation or settling tank, where most solids sink to the bottom and are removed. The sand filter removes any remaining solids before the water is chlorinated and pumped to a tank at the top of a water tower. The tank is raised so that water flows from it at high pressure, ready for people to use.

Below: Sewage passes first through a coarse screening tank which removes bulky solids, and then to a settling tank which removes grit. The primary sedimentation tank allows

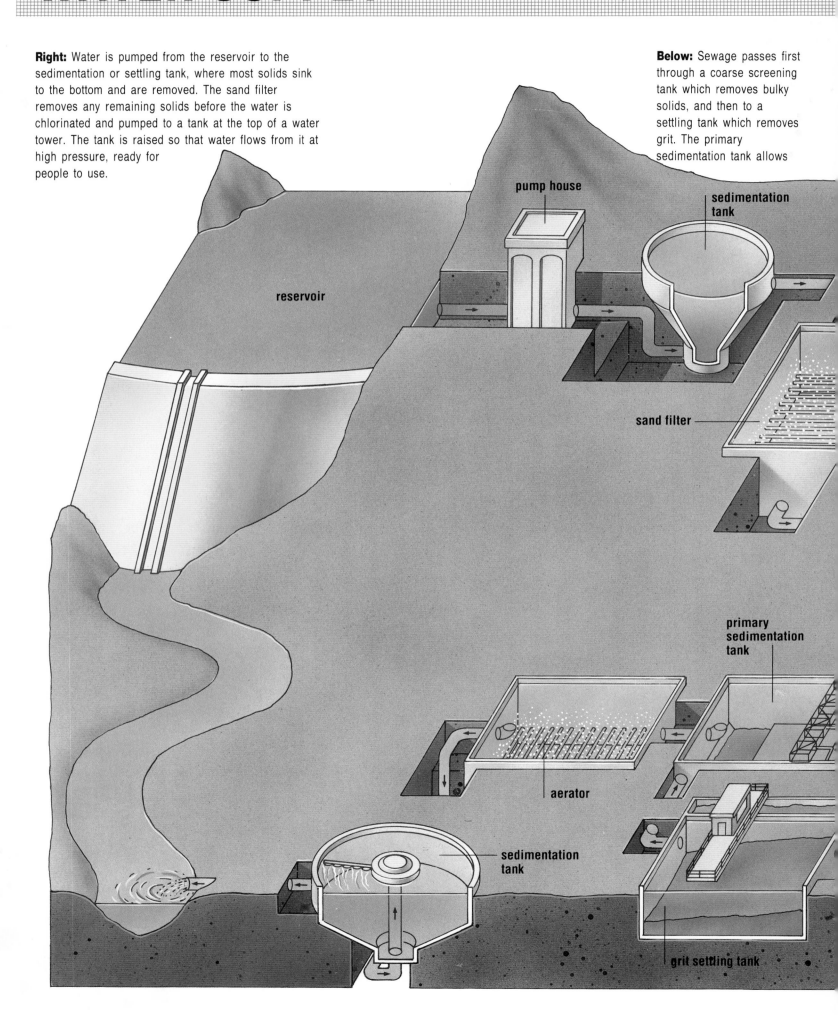

pump house

sedimentation tank

reservoir

sand filter

primary sedimentation tank

aerator

sedimentation tank

grit settling tank

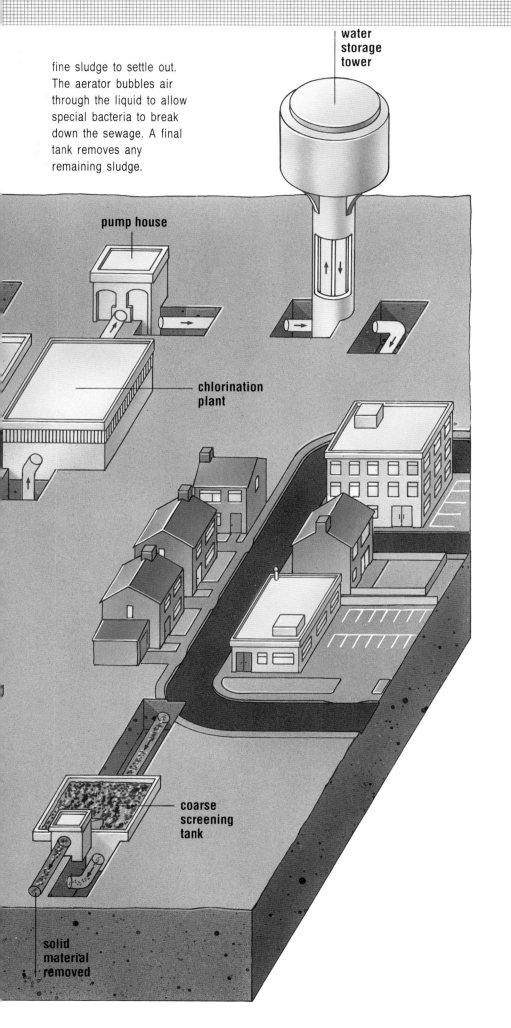

fine sludge to settle out. The aerator bubbles air through the liquid to allow special bacteria to break down the sewage. A final tank removes any remaining sludge.

water storage tower

pump house

chlorination plant

coarse screening tank

solid material removed

Towns and cities usually get their water from large reservoirs in which water is trapped behind a dam. The water in the reservoirs is not safe to drink. It must be purified at the waterworks before being pumped through pipes to our homes.

The first stage in water purification is called flocculation. This is carried out by adding chemicals such as alum to the water. These chemicals cause impurities to form into particles called flocs. When these have formed, the water is pumped into settling tanks, where most of the particles sink to the bottom and are removed.

Most of the remaining impurities are removed in the next stage, sand filtration. In this process, the water is pumped into a tank which has a bed of fine sand at the bottom. The water filters through the sand, leaving impurities behind. It then goes on to the final stage, chlorination. In this process, chlorine gas is bubbled through the water and kills any bacteria or germs remaining in it.

Waste water from our homes goes through the sewers to the sewage works. Here, the sewage goes first into a tank where solid materials are allowed to settle to the bottom, and are then removed. The remaining liquid is pumped into a tank where bacteria are added. The bacteria eat or digest the sewage, turning it into water and gas. After about eight hours, the water is pure enough to go back into a river or the sea.

The solid material removed from the first tank is also digested by bacteria. The resulting gas can be used to power generators, producing electricity to run the works. The left-over sludge can be used as agricultural fertilizer.

THE ELECTRIC MOTOR

Below: A universal electric motor, which will run on both direct and alternating current. The central part, called the rotor, contains several coils. Each coil is connected to different sections of the commutator. The stator, or stationary coil, provides the magnetic field which makes the rotor turn.

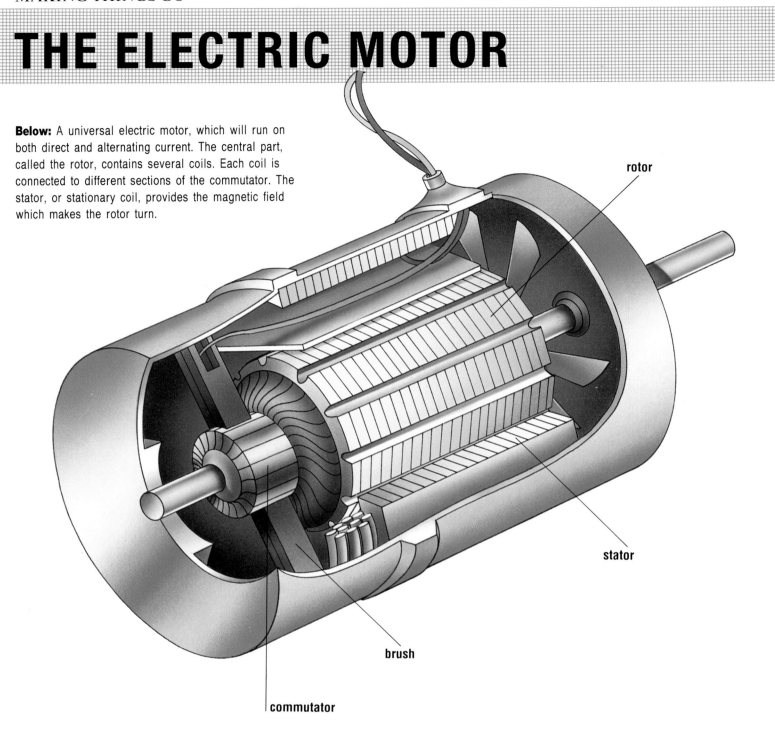

rotor

stator

brush

commutator

Electric motors are widely used in both industry and the home. They are found in electric locomotives and submarines, in food mixers and electric toothbrushes, in industrial robots and cranes. They are so useful because they convert electricity – a clean, convenient source of power – into movement.

There are many different kinds of electric motor. Some use DC, or direct current, electricity, and some use AC, or alternating current, electricity. DC is the type of electricity produced by batteries. It flows in one direction all the time. AC is the type of electricity produced by power stations. It reverses its direction of flow many times a second.

All electric motors work because electricity produces magnetic effects. In the simplest DC motors, a coil of wire is placed between the poles of a permanent magnet. When electricity flows through the coil, the coil itself becomes magnetized. The magnetized coil is twisted around by the permanent magnet.

In simple DC motors, the electric current has to be supplied to the coil through a device called a commutator. The commutator

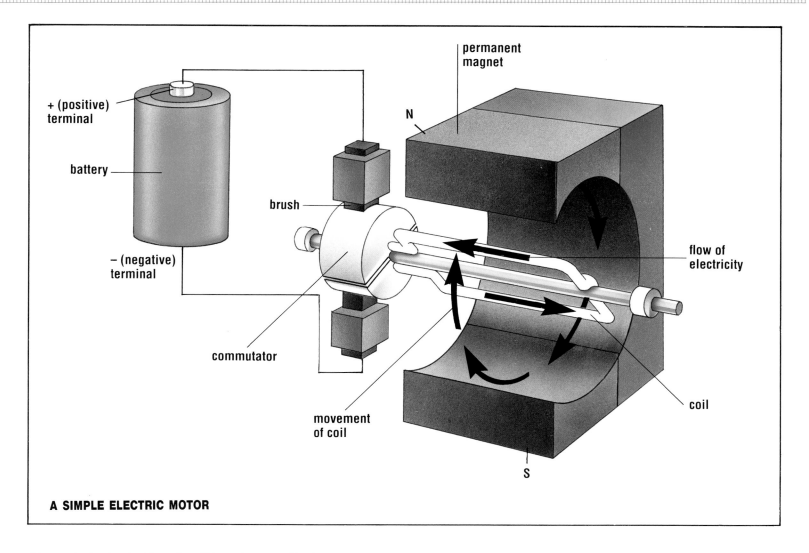

A SIMPLE ELECTRIC MOTOR

Labels: + (positive) terminal, battery, – (negative) terminal, brush, commutator, movement of coil, permanent magnet, N, flow of electricity, coil, S

Above: A simple electric motor. This motor uses direct current from a battery, and a permanent magnet. If the connections to the battery were reversed, the coil would turn in the opposite direction.

consists of two half circles of metal attached to the ends of the coil. The wires connecting the electric battery to the coil press against the half circles of metal, resulting in the reversal of the current after the coil has made half a rotation. If there was not a commutator, the coil would come to rest in a horizontal position after half a turn.

In larger motors, there is not just one coil but a series of coils, each displaced by a small angle from the previous one. The commutator, too, has many segments, one segment for each of the coils.

Above: Electric motors are used in electric trains. The electricity is picked up from a "third rail" laid alongside the usual pair of rails, or from an overhead cable. France's TGVs travel at over 160 miles per hour on specially built track.

THE GASOLINE ENGINE

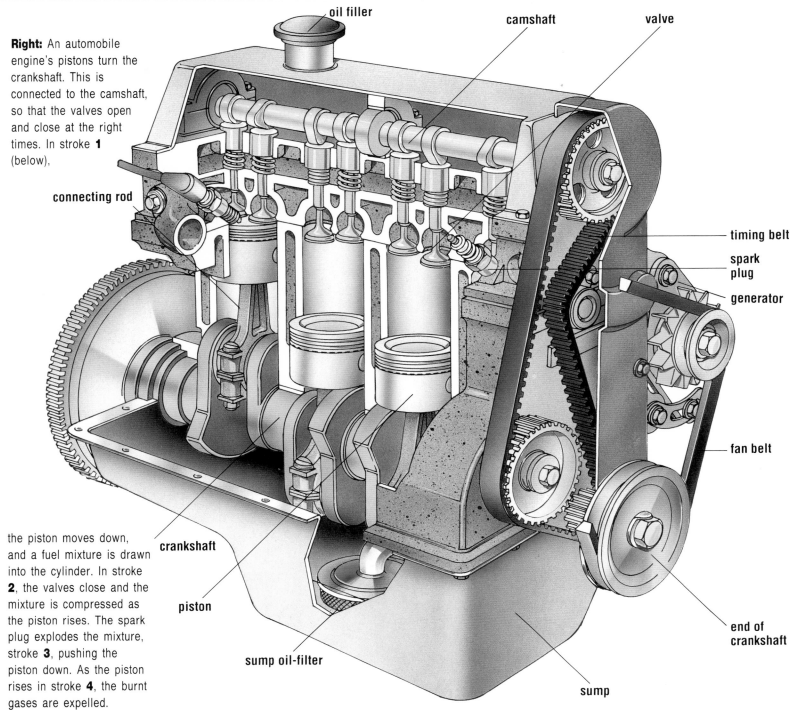

oil filler

camshaft

valve

Right: An automobile engine's pistons turn the crankshaft. This is connected to the camshaft, so that the valves open and close at the right times. In stroke **1** (below),

connecting rod

timing belt

spark plug

generator

fan belt

the piston moves down, and a fuel mixture is drawn into the cylinder. In stroke **2**, the valves close and the mixture is compressed as the piston rises. The spark plug explodes the mixture, stroke **3**, pushing the piston down. As the piston rises in stroke **4**, the burnt gases are expelled.

crankshaft

piston

sump oil-filter

end of crankshaft

sump

THE FOUR-STROKE ENGINE

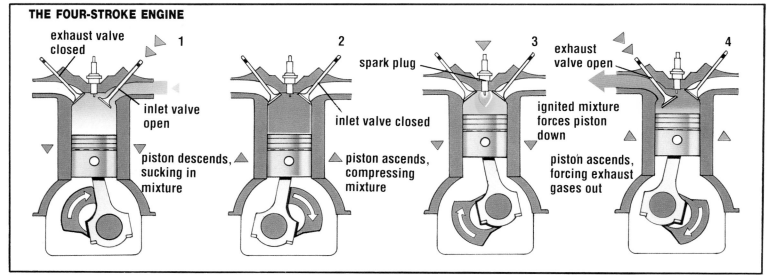

exhaust valve closed

1

inlet valve open

piston descends, sucking in mixture

2

spark plug

inlet valve closed

piston ascends, compressing mixture

3

ignited mixture forces piston down

exhaust valve open

4

piston ascends, forcing exhaust gases out

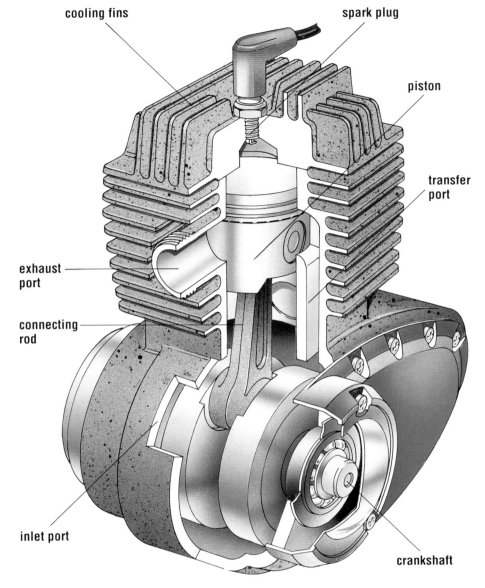

cooling fins

spark plug

piston

transfer
port

exhaust
port

connecting
rod

inlet port

crankshaft

Above: The two-stroke engine is small and powerful. However, it produces fumes and pollution because unburnt fuel is mixed with the exhaust gases. In stroke **1** (below), the piston rises, sucking the fuel mixture into the lower part of the engine through the inlet port. The rising piston compresses the fuel mixture already in the cylinder. A spark explodes the mixture when it is fully compressed. During stroke **2**, the piston descends, pushing a new fuel mixture through the transfer port into the cylinder. The burnt fuel is forced out through the exhaust.

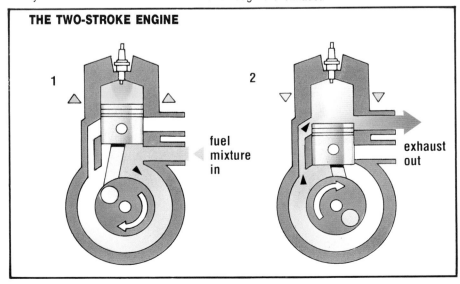

THE TWO-STROKE ENGINE

1

2

fuel
mixture
in

exhaust
out

The gasoline engine is sometimes called an "internal combustion engine" because fuel is burnt inside it ("combustion" means burning). Gasoline, a liquid made from crude oil, is the fuel most commonly used because it burns easily when mixed with air. Some internal combustion engines use a heavier type of fuel called diesel oil.

Inside a gasoline engine, a cylindrical piece of metal, called a piston, moves up and down inside a tight-fitting tube, called a cylinder. When the piston moves upward, it compresses (squeezes) a mixture of gasoline and air. The gasoline and air mixture enters the tube through holes, called ports, near the top of the tube. The ports are opened and closed by "doors" called valves.

When the mixture is fully compressed, a spark is produced by a spark plug near the top of the tube. The mixture explodes, and the gases produced expand rapidly, pushing the piston down the tube. The movement of the piston is used to turn the wheels of a car, motorcycle, or other vehicle.

Most cars have a four-stroke engine. These engines produce their power with four movements, or strokes, of the piston. Many motorcycles have a simpler type of engine called the two-stroke engine. This uses two movements of the piston to produce its power.

A diesel engine is similar to a four-stroke engine, but only air enters through the ports. The diesel oil fuel is squirted into the tube after the air has been compressed. The compressed air is so hot that a spark plug is not needed to explode the fuel and air mixture. This is known as "compression-ignition."

THE JET ENGINE

The jet engine used to power large airliners is called a gas turbine. In a gas turbine, a hot expanding gas flows at high speed over the blades of a type of "windmill," called a turbine, causing the blades to turn. These engines are used to drive ships and automobiles, to run electricity generators, and to pump gas through pipelines.

The type of gas turbine engine used in airliners is called a turbofan engine or jet engine. It works in the following way. First, air is drawn into the front of the engine by a large rotating fan. Some of the air passes into a compressor, where it is compressed (squeezed), before passing into a combustion chamber. Then fuel, such as aviation kerosene, is squirted in and ignited in the combustion chamber. The fuel and air mixture burns fiercely, producing hot gases at high temperature and pressure. These gases expand, rushing toward the back of the engine. As the gases stream backward, the engine, and the craft it is attached to, is forced forward. It is not, as often thought, the gases streaming out from the exhaust pipe of a jet which move the airplane along. The actual thrust in fact occurs *inside* the engine, pushing it forward, while the exhaust pipe serves only to allow the exhaust gases to escape.

Before emerging from the engine, the gases pass through a turbine, making it spin rapidly. The revolving turbine turns an axle which drives the compressor and the intake fan.

Some of the air taken in at the front of the engine bypasses the compressor, the combustion chamber, and the turbine. Instead, this air is sent straight to the rear of the engine, to keep it cool and quiet.

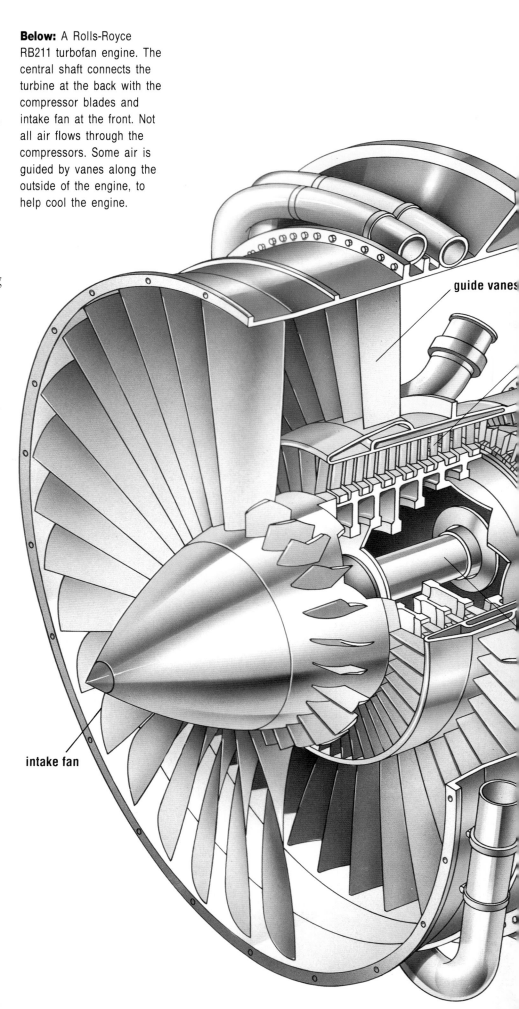

Below: A Rolls-Royce RB211 turbofan engine. The central shaft connects the turbine at the back with the compressor blades and intake fan at the front. Not all air flows through the compressors. Some air is guided by vanes along the outside of the engine, to help cool the engine.

guide vanes

intake fan

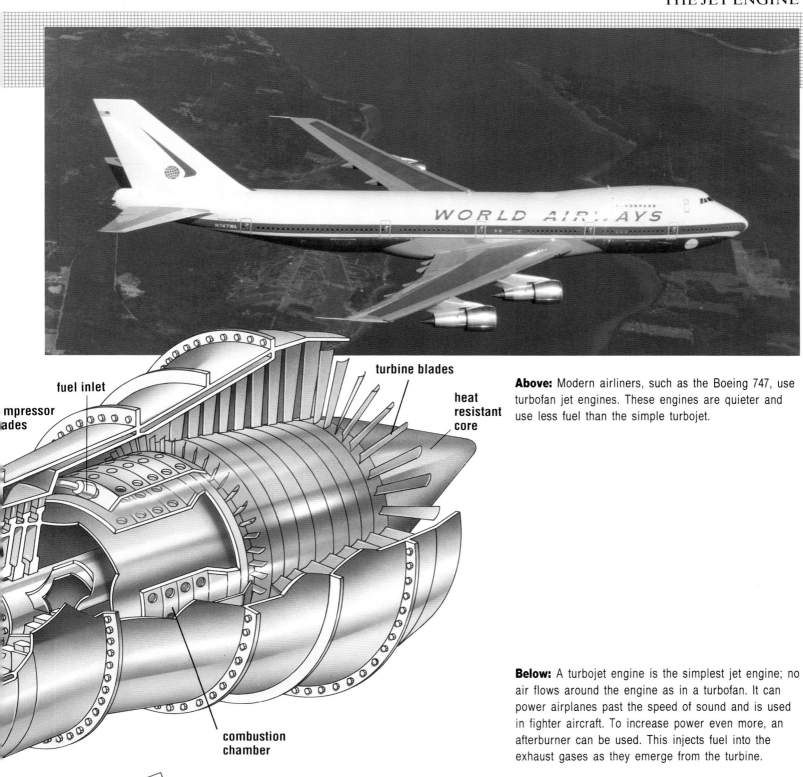

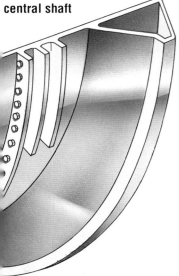

fuel inlet

compressor blades

turbine blades

heat resistant core

combustion chamber

central shaft

Above: Modern airliners, such as the Boeing 747, use turbofan jet engines. These engines are quieter and use less fuel than the simple turbojet.

Below: A turbojet engine is the simplest jet engine; no air flows around the engine as in a turbofan. It can power airplanes past the speed of sound and is used in fighter aircraft. To increase power even more, an afterburner can be used. This injects fuel into the exhaust gases as they emerge from the turbine.

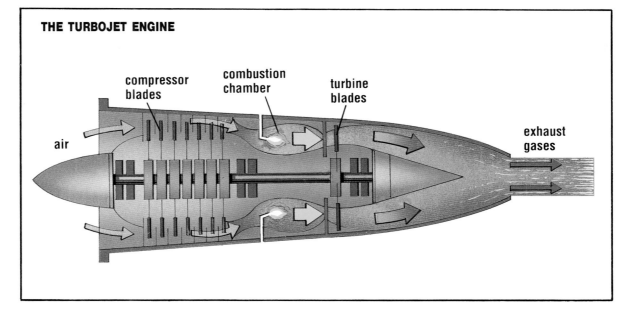

THE TURBOJET ENGINE

compressor blades

combustion chamber

turbine blades

air

exhaust gases

THE AUTOMOBILE

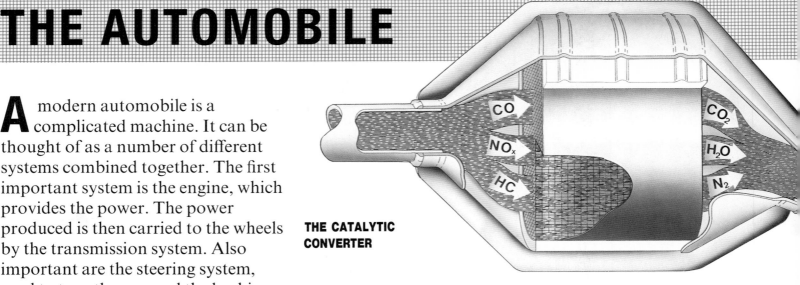

A modern automobile is a complicated machine. It can be thought of as a number of different systems combined together. The first important system is the engine, which provides the power. The power produced is then carried to the wheels by the transmission system. Also important are the steering system, used to turn the car, and the braking system, which stops the car. Finally, the suspension system supports the car and produces a smooth ride over rough roads, and the electrical system provides electricity and carries it around the car.

The transmission system consists of the clutch, gearbox, propeller shaft and differential gear. The gearbox, connected to the clutch and engine, converts the rapid movements produced by the engine to the slower movements that are needed to turn the wheels. The clutch is used to disconnect the engine from the gearbox while the gears are changed. The propeller shaft carries the power from the gearbox to the wheels through the differential gear, a device located in the middle of the rear axle which ensures that the rear wheels turn at a different speed to each other when a car goes around corners, to prevent skidding.

The braking system makes use of hydraulic or fluid power. When the driver presses on the brake pedal, the force is carried by levers to a cylinder of oil. The oil transmits the force through pipes to the brakes on the wheels. Here the oil pressure forces the brake pads against the wheels and slows them down.

The steering system consists of the steering wheel and a set of levers and cogwheels connecting the steering wheel to the front wheels of the car.

THE CATALYTIC CONVERTER

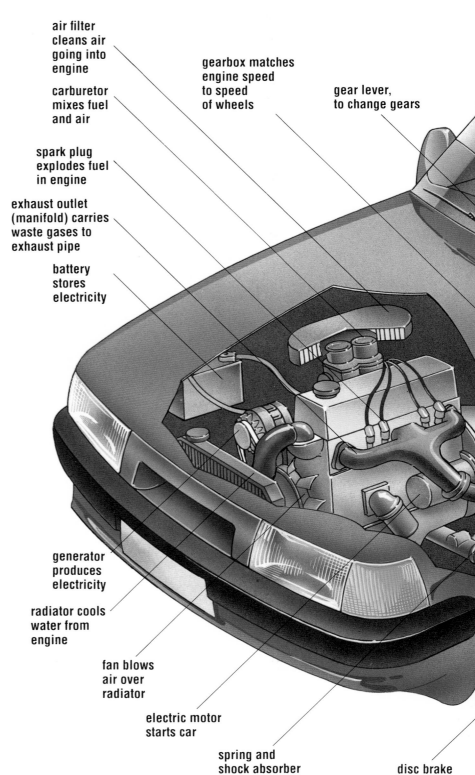

air filter cleans air going into engine

carburetor mixes fuel and air

spark plug explodes fuel in engine

exhaust outlet (manifold) carries waste gases to exhaust pipe

battery stores electricity

gearbox matches engine speed to speed of wheels

gear lever, to change gears

generator produces electricity

radiator cools water from engine

fan blows air over radiator

electric motor starts car

spring and shock absorber

disc brake

Left: A catalytic converter is a unit, about the size of a soccer ball, that fits into the exhaust system of an automobile. Inside is a honeycomb of metal coated with substances, such as platinum and palladium, which are called catalysts. These convert harmful gases in the exhaust, such as carbon monoxide (CO), nitrogen oxides (NO_x), and hydrocarbons (HC), into carbon dioxide (CO_2), water (H_2O) and nitrogen (N), which are not directly harmful.

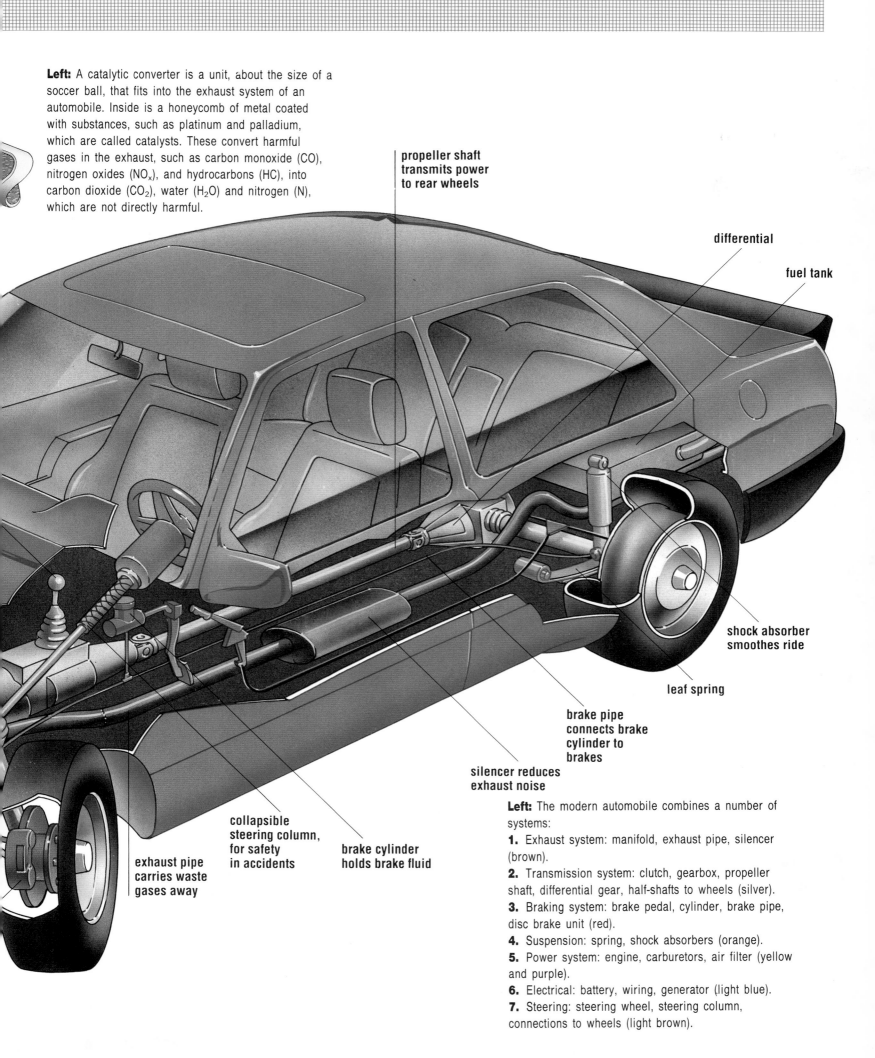

propeller shaft transmits power to rear wheels

differential

fuel tank

shock absorber smoothes ride

leaf spring

brake pipe connects brake cylinder to brakes

silencer reduces exhaust noise

collapsible steering column, for safety in accidents

brake cylinder holds brake fluid

exhaust pipe carries waste gases away

Left: The modern automobile combines a number of systems:

1. Exhaust system: manifold, exhaust pipe, silencer (brown).

2. Transmission system: clutch, gearbox, propeller shaft, differential gear, half-shafts to wheels (silver).

3. Braking system: brake pedal, cylinder, brake pipe, disc brake unit (red).

4. Suspension: spring, shock absorbers (orange).

5. Power system: engine, carburetors, air filter (yellow and purple).

6. Electrical: battery, wiring, generator (light blue).

7. Steering: steering wheel, steering column, connections to wheels (light brown).

THE MOTORCYCLE

Right: A modern motorcycle often has a multi-cylinder engine. The cylinders can be arranged side by side, end to end, or in a V-shape. The size of the engine is measured in cubic centimetres ("cc"). Large touring bikes may have 1,000cc engines. The smallest bikes have engines of only 50cc.

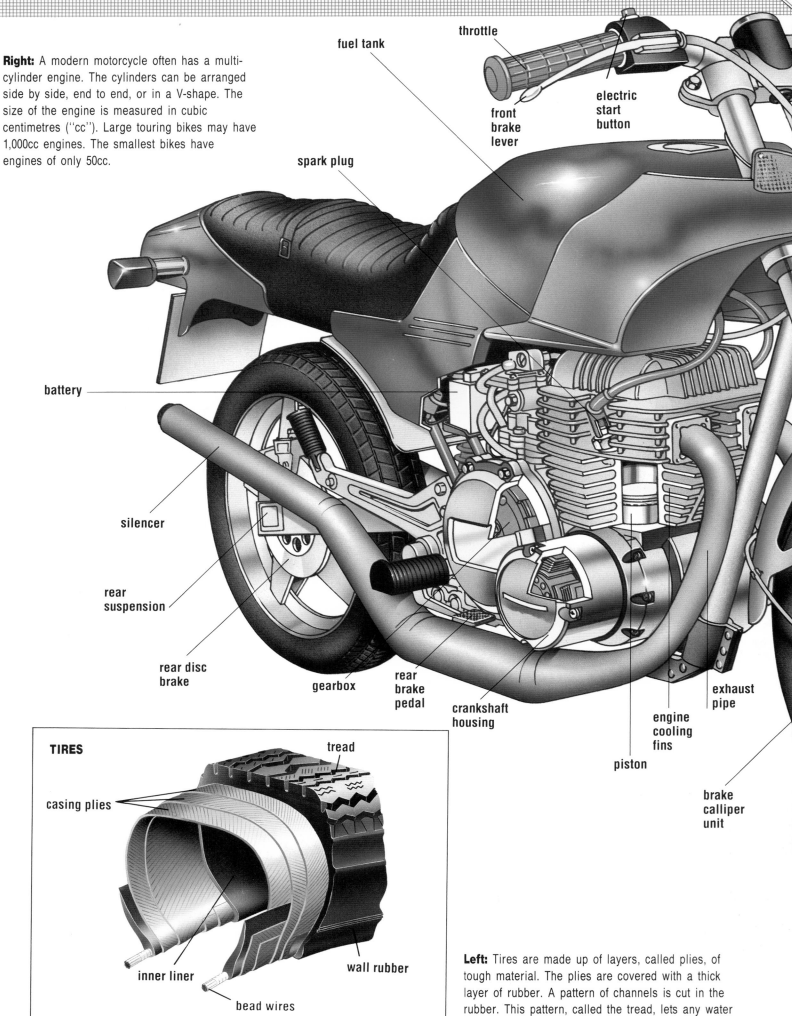

throttle

fuel tank

electric start button

front brake lever

spark plug

battery

silencer

rear suspension

rear disc brake

gearbox

rear brake pedal

crankshaft housing

piston

engine cooling fins

exhaust pipe

brake calliper unit

TIRES

tread

casing plies

inner liner

bead wires

wall rubber

Left: Tires are made up of layers, called plies, of tough material. The plies are covered with a thick layer of rubber. A pattern of channels is cut in the rubber. This pattern, called the tread, lets any water under the tire drain away.

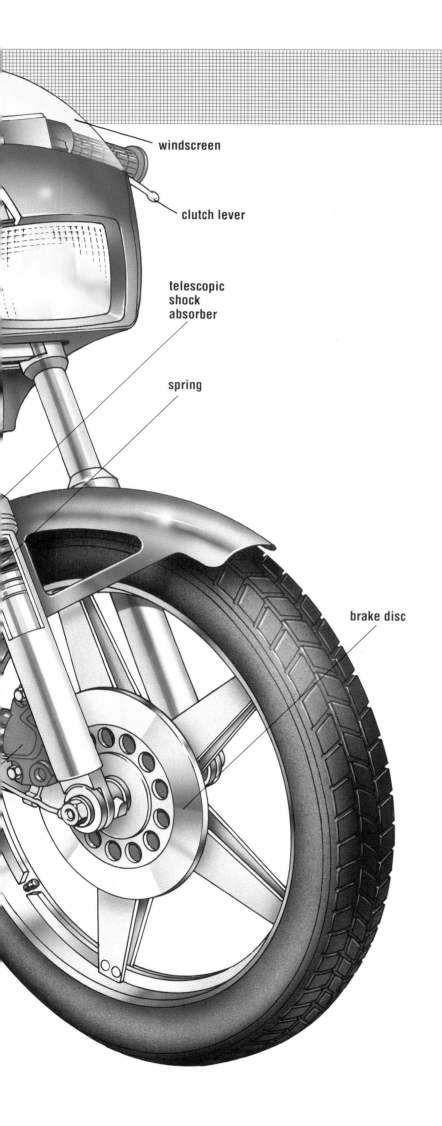

windscreen

clutch lever

telescopic
shock
absorber

spring

brake disc

The first motorcycle was built in 1869 by two French brothers, Ernest and Pierre Michaux. They did this by attaching a small steam engine behind the saddle of a bicycle, which must have given the rider a rather hot seat! It was not until 1901 that another pair of French brothers, Michel and Eugène Werner, produced an improved machine with a modern layout. It had the engine fixed low down between the wheels, and the fuel tank above the engine. This layout made the machine easier to control because it was no longer top-heavy and therefore did not tip up. Other manufacturers quickly adopted this design, and modern motorcycles still use it.

Small motorcycles usually have small, single-cylinder, two-stroke engines. Larger machines often have four-cylinder, four-stroke engines. The larger the engine, the more powerful it is.

The engine is connected to the clutch and gearbox. As in an automobile, the gearbox is used to reduce the speed of the engine's movement. This allows the fast-turning engine to be connected to the slow-moving wheels. The clutch disconnects the engine from the gearbox when the gears are changed. A chain or belt carries the power from the gearbox to the back wheel.

The steering system is particularly simple on a motorcycle. The front wheel is held between a metal fork which can be turned by moving the handlebars. The suspension, used to smooth the ride, is simple, too. Shock absorbers connected to the wheels contain coiled springs which compress as the machine goes over bumps in the road.

ELECTRIC VEHICLES

Right: Electric vehicles are used today mainly as delivery vans in towns and cities. They are quiet and pollution free. Their lack of speed and short range is not important for short journeys.

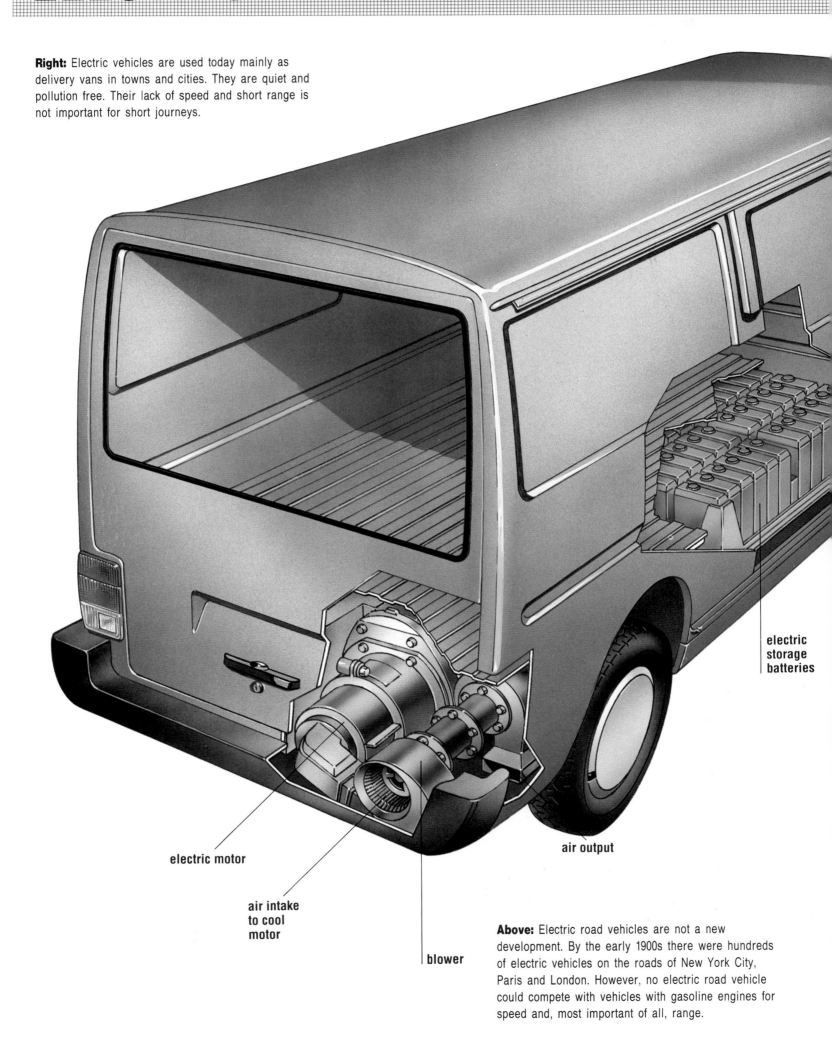

electric
storage
batteries

electric motor

air output

air intake
to cool
motor

blower

Above: Electric road vehicles are not a new development. By the early 1900s there were hundreds of electric vehicles on the roads of New York City, Paris and London. However, no electric road vehicle could compete with vehicles with gasoline engines for speed and, most important of all, range.

Some automobiles, trucks, and trains are powered by electricity rather than by a gasoline or diesel engine. These electric vehicles do not produce harmful fumes like gasoline-powered vehicles. They are also quieter and simpler to build. Unfortunately, they are also slow and cannot travel long distances.

There are two types of electric vehicle. The first type, which includes electric trains and fairground dodgem cars, is continuously fed electric power from an electrified rail or overhead cable. The other type of electric vehicle carries its own electricity, stored in batteries. In both types, the electricity is fed to a powerful electric motor which turns the wheels.

The battery most commonly used in battery-driven vehicles is the lead-acid type. This is the same as those used in gasoline-driven cars to provide electricity for the starter motor and for the lights when parked. It consists of sheets of lead and lead oxide standing in a strong acid. When electricity is fed into the battery, it produces chemical changes in the lead and lead oxide, which then store the electricity. Later, the stored electricity can be released. The problem with battery-driven vehicles is that the batteries are heavy. Scientists have looked for lighter, more efficient batteries but, so far, without success.

The performance of electric vehicles can be considerably improved by using light materials in their construction. The vehicles can also be streamlined effectively so that the air does not hold them back as they move along. Some vehicles also conserve electricity by charging the battery when braking. The speed of the vehicle is used to turn an electric generator as the vehicle slows.

Right: The Sunraycer holds the world record for the fastest solar-powered vehicle. It uses solar cells on its top and sides to convert energy from the sun into electricity, which drives its electric motors. In 1988 it reached a speed of 49 miles per hour in Arizona. In 1987, Sunraycer won a race for solar-powered cars from Darwin in the north of Australia to Adelaide in the south, a distance of over 1,800 miles. It completed the race in six days, two days quicker than the next vehicle.

THE LOCOMOTIVE

The first locomotives, also called railroad engines, were powered by steam. Today, most railroads use diesel engines, although some are electrically powered.

In a steam engine, coal is burned in a furnace. The hot gases produced pass along tubes in the boiler and heat water, producing steam. The steam goes through a regulator valve which is used by the driver to control the speed of the engine. It is then heated again (superheated) to a very high temperature, and its pressure rises too. The steam is then sent to the engine's cylinder. Inside the cylinder, the high-pressure steam expands and forces a piston along the cylinder. The piston is connected to the wheels by a series of rods, and thus the movement of the cylinder makes the wheels move. The steam then leaves the piston and passes up the chimney,

creating a draft that helps keep the furnace burning fiercely.

A diesel railroad engine is really a combination of a diesel engine and an electric motor. A diesel engine is used to drive a generator which produces electricity. The electricity produced is fed to electric motors connected to the wheels. Diesel locomotives have two main advantages over steam engines. Firstly, they are always ready for use, whereas it takes a long time to heat the water in a steam engine. Secondly, a diesel locomotive can travel greater distances as it does not need to take water on board.

Electric trains, which draw their power from overhead electricity cables or from an electrified track, are expensive to build. They are only used in areas where the high number of passengers can justify the expense of building the special track.

Below: The steam produced in the boiler of a steam engine flows into the cylinder forcing the piston along. When the piston reaches the end of the cylinder, the piston valve moves, directing the steam into the other end of the cylinder. The piston is forced back to its original position, and the cycle repeats. The wheels are connected to the piston by connecting rods.

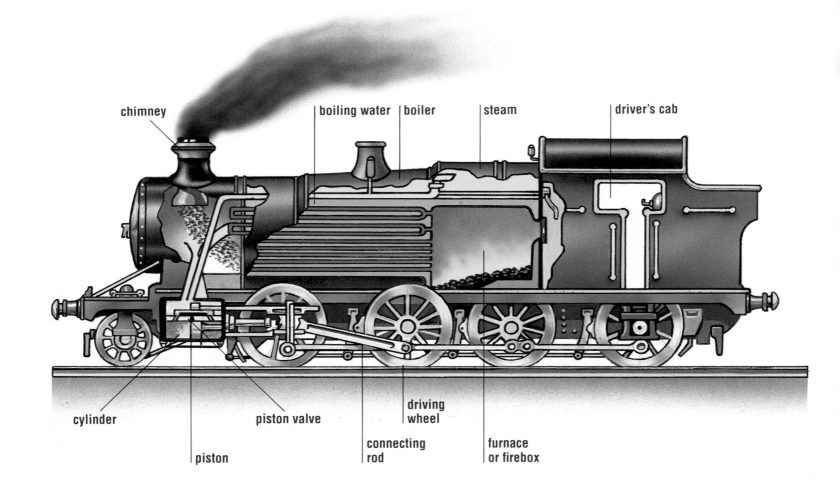

chimney   boiling water   boiler   steam   driver's cab

cylinder   piston valve   driving wheel

piston   connecting rod   furnace or firebox

Below: The traction, or driving, motors lie between the wheels of a diesel railroad engine. These are electric motors powered by electricity produced by the generator and the diesel engine.

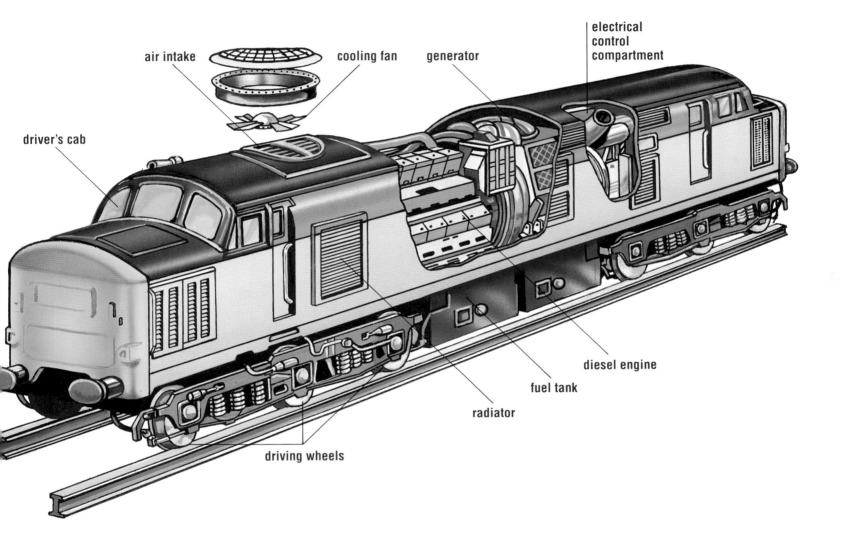

air intake

cooling fan

generator

electrical
control
compartment

driver's cab

diesel engine

fuel tank

radiator

driving wheels

Right: In many big cities, electric trains are used to carry passengers under the ground. Electric trains, which collect their electricity from special tracks or cables, are very good for journeys where the train has to stop and start frequently.

ELECTRIC TRAINS

THE AIRPLANE

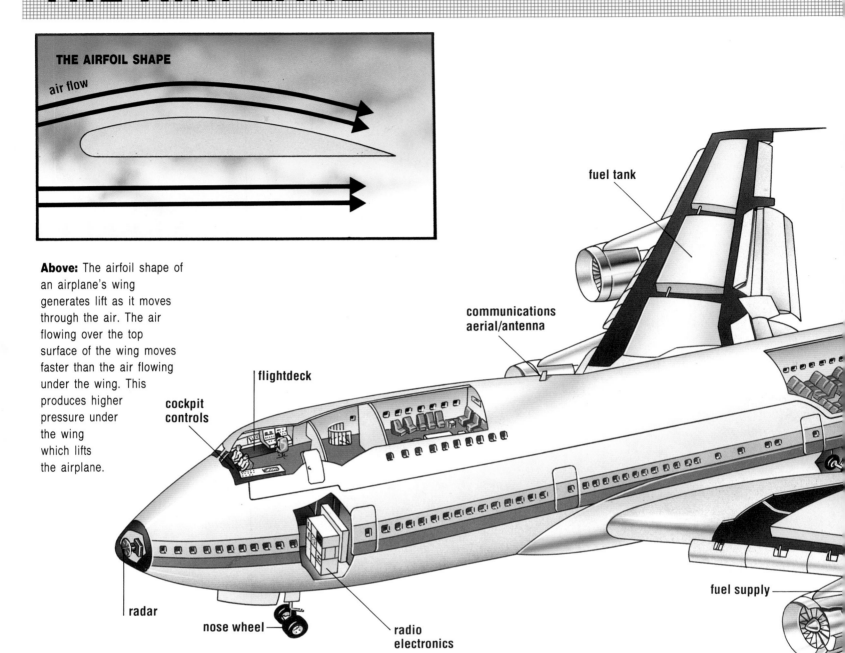

THE AIRFOIL SHAPE

air flow

Above: The airfoil shape of an airplane's wing generates lift as it moves through the air. The air flowing over the top surface of the wing moves faster than the air flowing under the wing. This produces higher pressure under the wing which lifts the airplane.

fuel tank

communications aerial/antenna

flightdeck

cockpit controls

radar

nose wheel

radio electronics

fuel supply

How does an airplane stay in the air? The answer is that it is all due to the shape of its wings. The wings of an airplane have a special shape called an airfoil, which is curved on the top and almost flat underneath. When an airplane is in flight, air flows over the wings in such a way that there is greater pressure below than above them. This produces an upward force called "lift." The wings are also attached to the body of the

airplane at a slight angle, so that the front edge of the wing is slightly higher than the back edge. As the plane moves along, air strikes the underside of the wing, producing some additional lift.

To help the airplane turn and gain height, there are hinged sections on the back edges of the wings and tail. The hinged sections on the small tail (rear) wings are called elevators. These can be moved up and down to

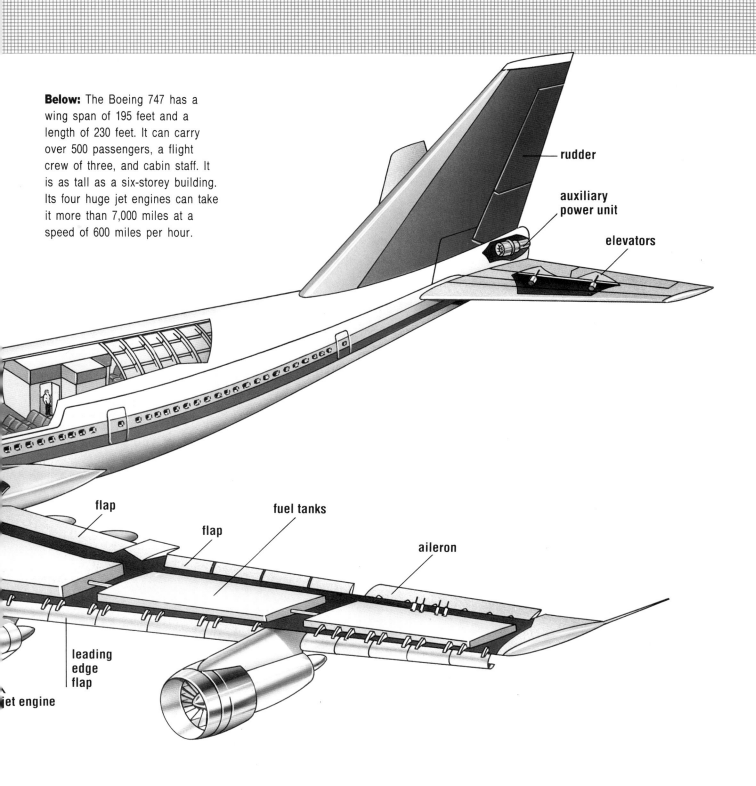

Below: The Boeing 747 has a wing span of 195 feet and a length of 230 feet. It can carry over 500 passengers, a flight crew of three, and cabin staff. It is as tall as a six-storey building. Its four huge jet engines can take it more than 7,000 miles at a speed of 600 miles per hour.

rudder

auxiliary power unit

elevators

flap

flap

fuel tanks

aileron

leading edge flap

jet engine

make the airplane climb or dive. On the main wings, there are hinged surfaces called ailerons, and on the tail fin there is a hinged rudder. Both the ailerons and the rudder are used to make turns.

To land safely, an airplane has to fly as slowly as possible. However, as the airplane slows down, the wings no longer produce as much lift. To overcome this, there are hinged surfaces called flaps on each wing,

between the ailerons and the body of the airplane. The flaps are lowered when landing to increase the lift of the wings.

Most small airplanes have a propeller to move them forward. The propeller pushes air backward as it rotates at high speed. This produces a forward thrust on the airplane. Larger airplanes, and high-performance military airplanes, are powered by jet engines.

THE HELICOPTER

The helicopter is an airplane with a difference, because it can hover and remain completely still in the air. It is able to do this because its wings continue to move through the air even when it is stationary.

The wings of a helicopter are the blades which turn all the time it is in the air. The blades of a helicopter have an airfoil shape like the wings of an airplane. Their top surface is curved, with the undersurface almost flat. As the blades turn, there is greater air pressure under the blades than above them, and this produces an upward lift force.

The amount of lift produced by the turning blades depends upon the pitch (angle) of the blades as they turn. If the front edge of a blade is higher than its back edge, it produces more lift than it would if it were flat. To take the helicopter up, the pilot increases the pitch of the blades. To take the helicopter down, the pilot decreases the pitch of the blades. To fly forward, the pilot changes the pitch of the blades as they turn. As each blade moves past the tail of the helicopter, the pitch is increased. Then, as the blade sweeps past the front of the helicopter, its pitch is decreased. The result is that the blades at the back of the helicopter produce more lift than those at the front. This moves the helicopter forward. To move backward or to one side, the pilot adjusts the pitch of the blades to produce more lift at the front or to one side.

Most helicopters have another set of blades at the back. These prevent the helicopter from spinning around in the air, in the opposite direction to the turning blades.

Right: The Westland/Aerospatiale Lynx is powered by two gas turbine engines and has a top speed of 180 miles per hour. The main rotor, or set of blades, is 42 feet across. The pilot and co-pilot each have a set of controls. The collective pitch level changes the pitch (angle) of all the main rotor blades at the same time. The cyclic pitch stick varies the pitch of the blades as they rotate. The tail rotor control pedals alter the pitch of the tail rotor.

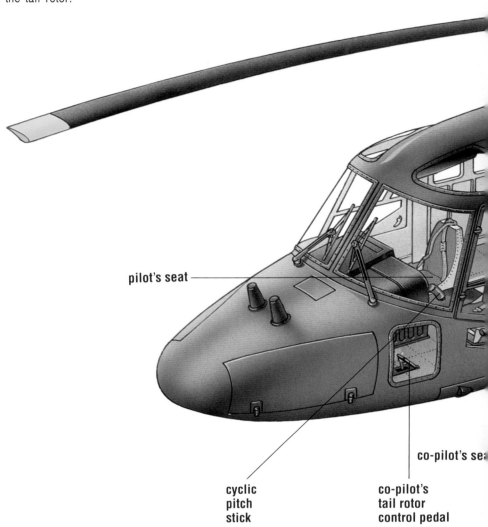

pilot's seat

co-pilot's se

cyclic pitch stick

co-pilot's tail rotor control pedal

Right: When taking off **(1)**, the collective pitch lever is pulled up. The lift produced by the blades becomes greater than the weight, and the helicopter rises. To move forward **(2)**, the cyclic pitch stick is pushed forward. This produces greater lift from the blades at the back, tilting the rotor to produce a forward force. To move backward **(3)**, the cyclic pitch stick is pulled back, tilting the rotor back to produce a backward force. To hover **(4)**, the lift must equal the weight.

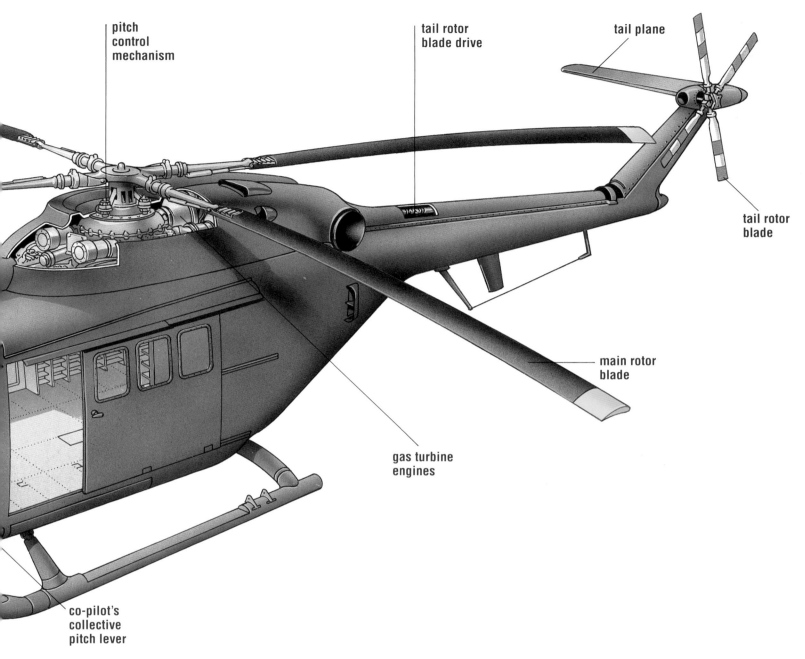

pitch
control
mechanism

tail rotor
blade drive

tail plane

tail rotor
blade

main rotor
blade

gas turbine
engines

co-pilot's
collective
pitch lever

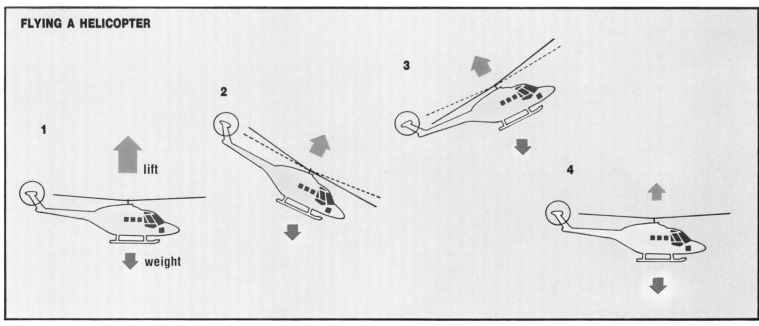

FLYING A HELICOPTER

1

lift

weight

2

3

4

THE SUBMARINE

The first successful submarine was built in 1620 by a Dutchman, Cornelius van Drebbel. It was made of greased leather stretched over a wooden frame. Oars poked out through the sides. This strange boat was successfully used on the River Thames, near London, in England.

periscopes

communications masts

radar masts

conning tower

hydroplane

torpedoes in racks

galley

officers's quarters

dining room

control and periscope room

bunks

recreation room

torpedo tubes

DIVING AND SURFACING

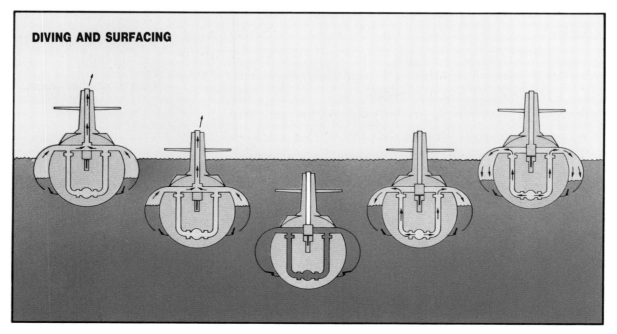

Left: With its ballast tanks empty, a submarine floats on the surface. To dive, seawater is pumped into the ballast tanks through valves near the bottom of the tanks. To dive more quickly, the propellers drive the submarine forward and the hydroplanes – horizontal fins – are angled to direct the craft downwards. To surface, compressed air is pumped into the ballast tanks, forcing the water out.

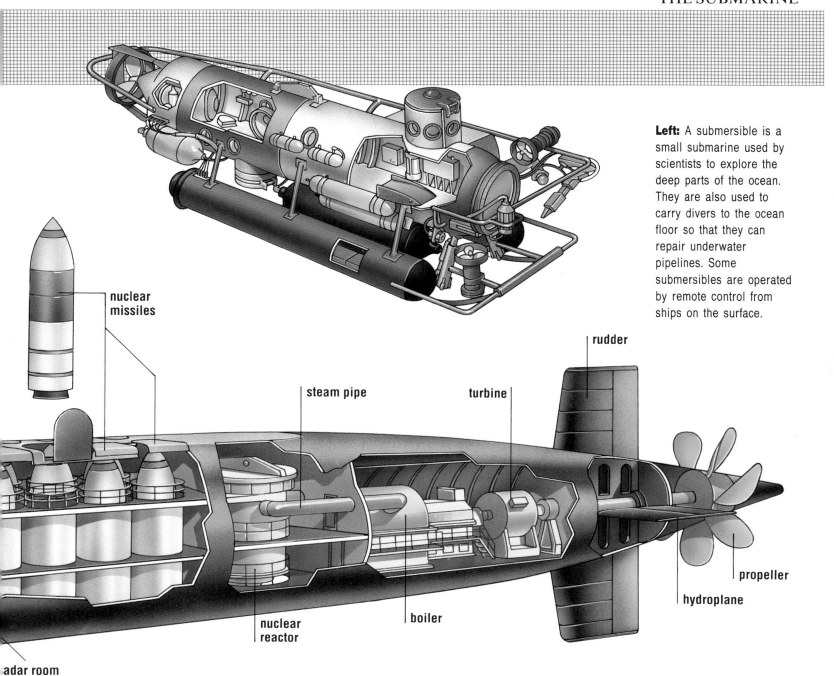

Left: A submersible is a small submarine used by scientists to explore the deep parts of the ocean. They are also used to carry divers to the ocean floor so that they can repair underwater pipelines. Some submersibles are operated by remote control from ships on the surface.

nuclear missiles

rudder

steam pipe

turbine

nuclear reactor

boiler

propeller

hydroplane

adar room

ditioner

Today, submarines are made with a long, cigar-shaped steel hull. On top of this is the conning tower, which holds the periscope and radio aerial. On the sides of some submarines are large ballast tanks. Other submarines have a second metal skin around the hull, with the ballast tanks between the skins. These tanks are used to make the submarine dive or surface. To dive, water is allowed to flow into the tanks, making the submarine heavier and causing it to sink. To surface, air is blown into the tanks, forcing some of the water out. As a result, the submarine is lighter and rises to the surface.

A nuclear submarine is powered by a nuclear reactor. This produces heat from uranium fuel. The heat is used to produce steam which is fed to a turbine and the turbine turns a propeller at the back of the submarine. The steam is then changed back into water and reused. The air in a submarine is reused, too, after it has been purified.

A nuclear submarine can travel completely around the world without surfacing. It finds its way underwater by using very accurate compasses based on gyroscopes, spinning metal wheels that can sense when the submarine changes direction. When the submarine surfaces, it is able to check the accuracy of the gyroscopes by using radio signals from satellites high above the Earth.

Above: A nuclear missile-carrying submarine. The missiles are carried in vertical containers set in two rows behind the conning tower. The hull has a rounded, hump-backed shape in order to accommodate the missiles.

THE HOVERCRAFT

The hovercraft is also known as an air-cushion vehicle (ACV), because as it moves along, it floats on a cushion of air. This means that a hovercraft never makes contact with the land or water surface it is traveling across. As a result, a hovercraft can move much faster than a normal ship. It is not held back by the drag of the water, or by waves and currents in the water. A hovercraft can also move equally easily over land, water, or rough, swampy country.

The hovercraft was invented in 1955 by Christopher Cockerell, a British engineer. He found that a cushion of air would form under a flat-bottomed boat if air was blown downward and inward through jets around the edge of the hull. He also found that a "skirt" of tough but flexible material around the edge of the hull helped to prevent the air cushion from escaping. The majority of modern hovercraft use the design Cockerell developed.

Most hovercraft are moved along by large propellers fixed to the upper decks. The same engines that power the fans pumping air under the craft often also turn the propellers. The thrust provided by the propellers can be varied to speed or slow the craft.

A hovercraft can be difficult to steer because there is so little friction between the craft and the surface it is traveling over. The craft is steered by swiveling the propellers, or by varying their power, and by using rudders at the stern (back). In addition, the entire craft can be tilted as it turns. This is done by reducing the pressure from the air jets on the side that is to be dipped. Even with these devices, hovercraft can be extremely difficult to steer in windy weather.

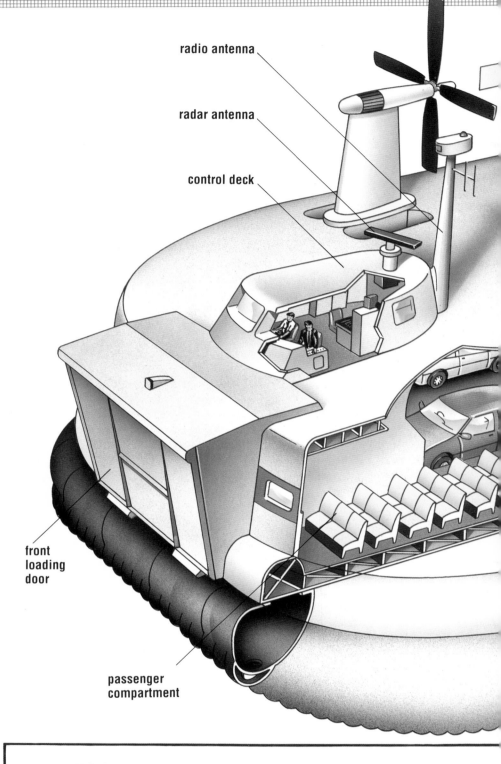

radio antenna

radar antenna

control deck

front loading door

passenger compartment

THE HYDROFOIL

Right: The hydrofoil is a boat that skims above the water, on wings. These special wings are called hydrofoils and are attached to the underside of the hull. They are shaped like airplane wings, with a curved upper surface and a flat lower surface. As the boat moves along, the hydrofoils provide lift in the same way as an airplane's wing. The boat is lifted above the surface of the water, and can move faster than a normal boat. There are several different hydrofoil designs. V-shaped foils (left) help to steady the craft as it moves along. They are used on passenger boats. Designs with separate hydrofoils (right) are better in rough seas because their angle can be adjusted to suit conditions.

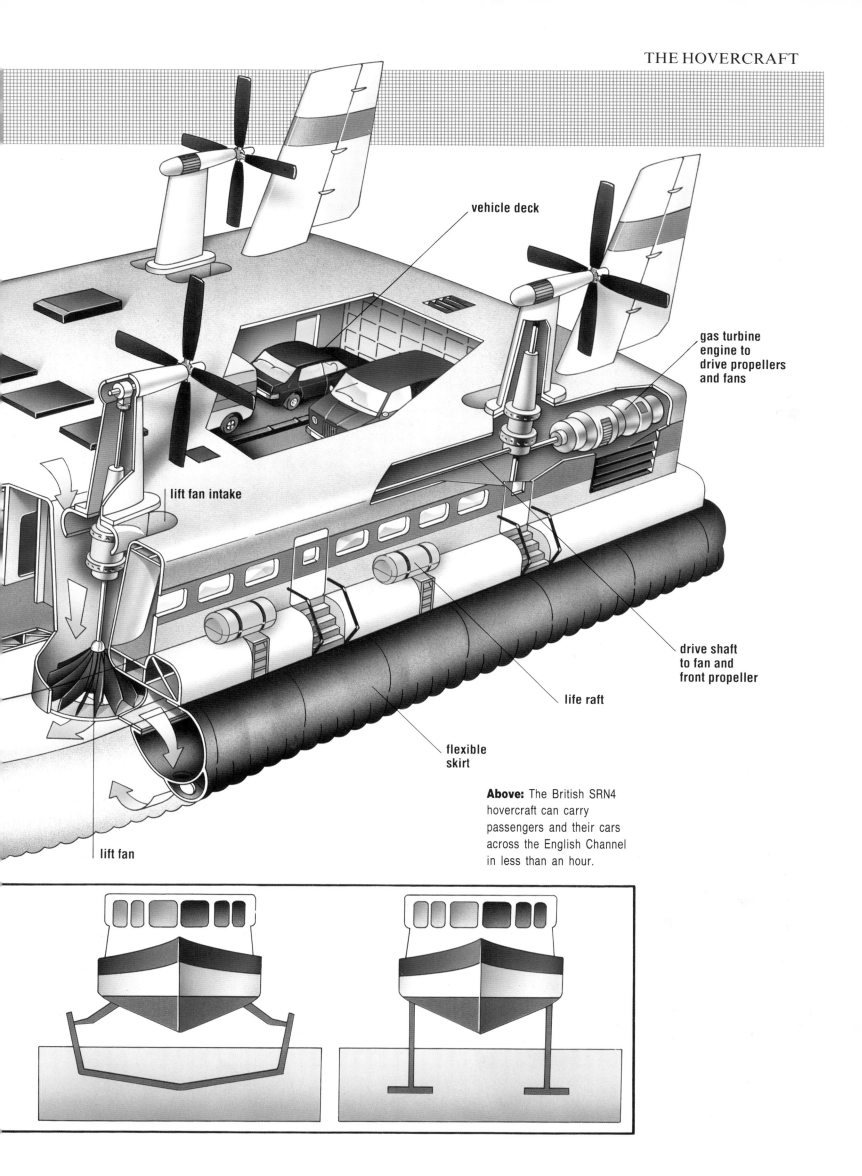

vehicle deck

gas turbine
engine to
drive propellers
and fans

lift fan intake

drive shaft
to fan and
front propeller

life raft

flexible
skirt

lift fan

Above: The British SRN4
hovercraft can carry
passengers and their cars
across the English Channel
in less than an hour.

THE SKYSCRAPER

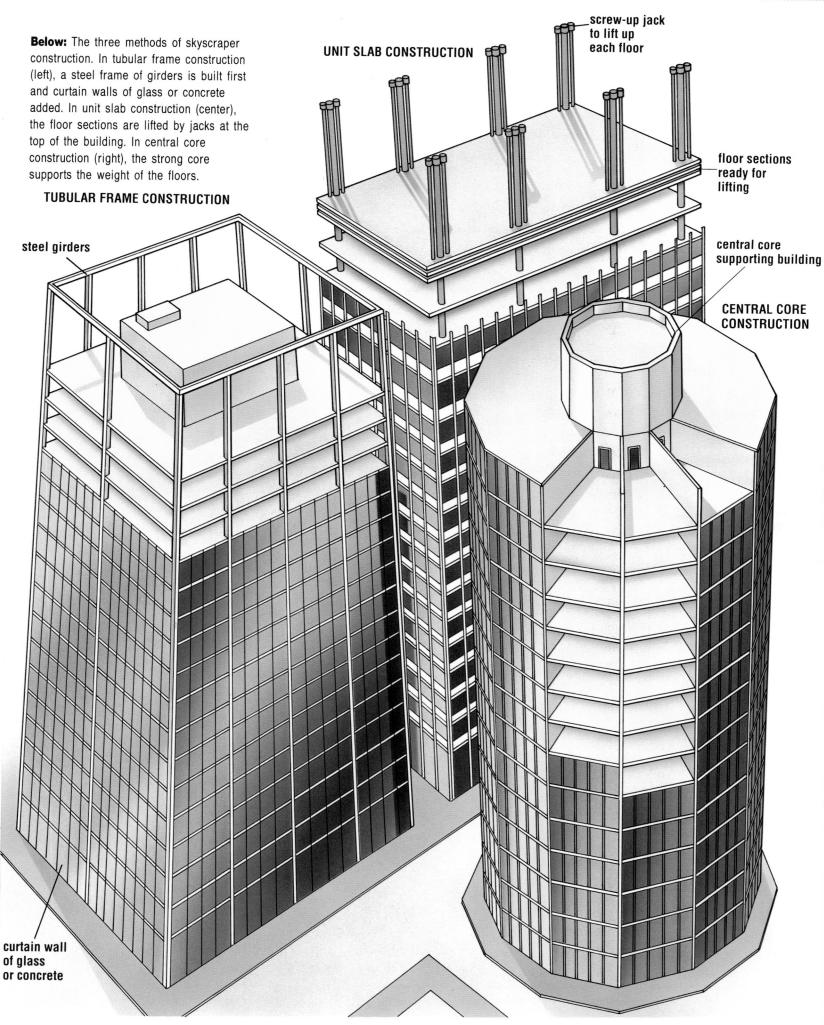

Below: The three methods of skyscraper construction. In tubular frame construction (left), a steel frame of girders is built first and curtain walls of glass or concrete added. In unit slab construction (center), the floor sections are lifted by jacks at the top of the building. In central core construction (right), the strong core supports the weight of the floors.

TUBULAR FRAME CONSTRUCTION

UNIT SLAB CONSTRUCTION

screw-up jack to lift up each floor

floor sections ready for lifting

central core supporting building

CENTRAL CORE CONSTRUCTION

steel girders

curtain wall of glass or concrete

screw-up jack

The tallest building in the world is the Sears Tower in Chicago, Ill. It has 110 storeys and rises to a height of 520 yards from the ground.

Skyscrapers such as the Sears Tower present their builders with many problems. Perhaps the most important of these is that of ensuring that the building is stable; it must not collapse whatever happens. For this reason, skyscrapers must have strong underground foundations. These are made by digging out the ground and filling the hole with concrete. If the ground is soft, the foundations must go deep into the earth.

There are three widely used methods of building skyscrapers: the unit slab frame method, the tubular frame method, and the central core method. In the unit slab method, each floor is added to the building on top of the lower ones. In the tubular frame method, a very strong steel or concrete frame is built first, then the walls and floors of the building are attached to the frame. In the central core method of construction, the elevators and staircases are enclosed in a strong central column. The skyscraper is built around this core.

Heating, air conditioning, electricity, water supply, drainage, and elevators are all difficult to instal in skyscrapers. Great lengths of pipes and cables are needed. There are nearly 65 miles of water pipes and 3,500 miles of telephone cables in the 102-storey Empire State Building in New York City, for example. In modern skyscrapers, complete floors are often given over to housing water tanks, air conditioning, and electrical machinery.

Below: An air conditioning unit. Air pumped from a room is mixed with fresh air from the outside. Then it is pumped through dust filters, heating and cooling units, a smell filter and a humidifier, and returned to the room.

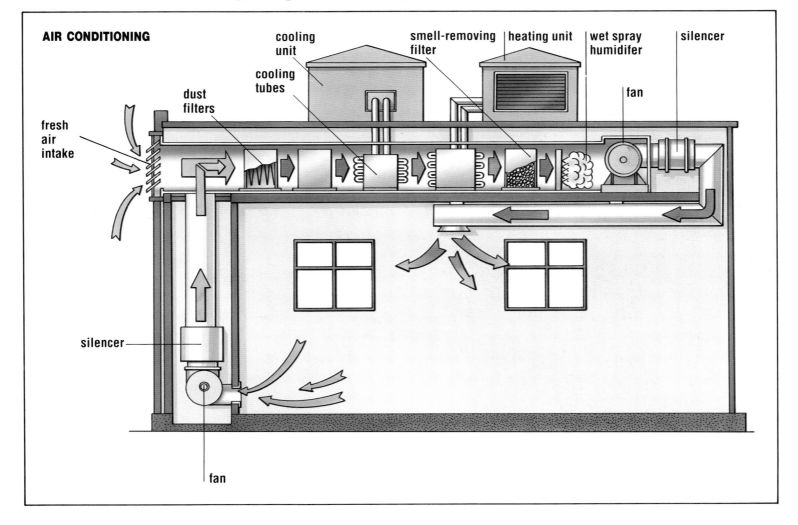

AIR CONDITIONING

cooling unit

cooling tubes

dust filters

fresh air intake

smell-removing filter

heating unit

wet spray humidifer

silencer

fan

silencer

fan

THE ELEVATOR AND ESCALATOR

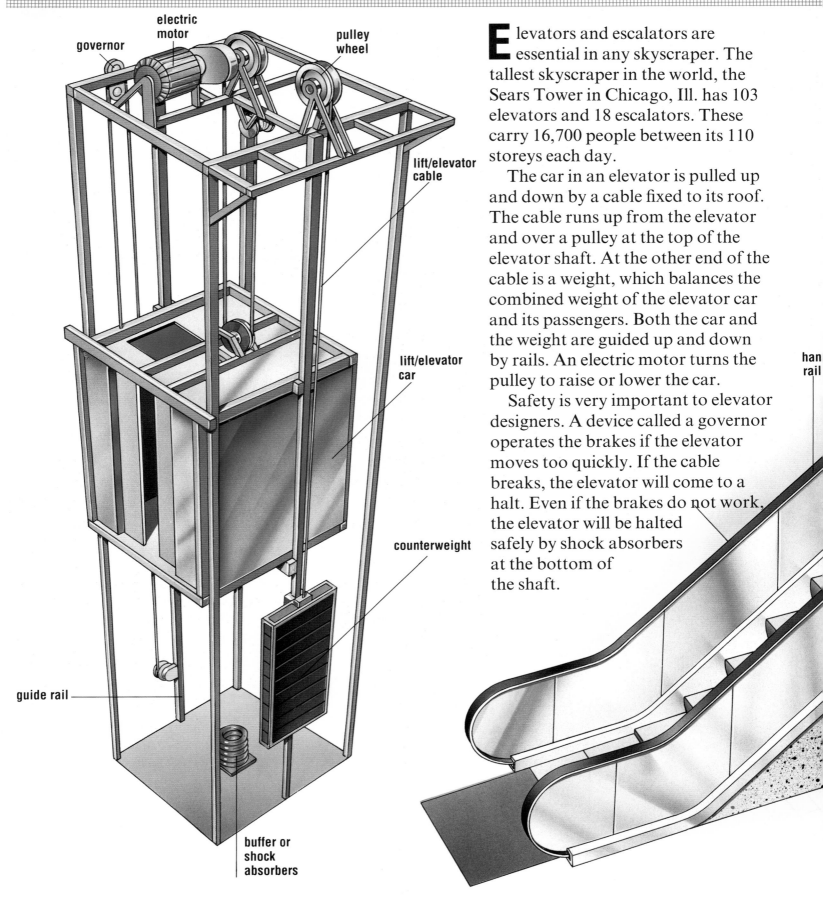

governor

electric motor

pulley wheel

lift/elevator cable

lift/elevator car

counterweight

guide rail

buffer or shock absorbers

han rail

Elevators and escalators are essential in any skyscraper. The tallest skyscraper in the world, the Sears Tower in Chicago, Ill. has 103 elevators and 18 escalators. These carry 16,700 people between its 110 storeys each day.

The car in an elevator is pulled up and down by a cable fixed to its roof. The cable runs up from the elevator and over a pulley at the top of the elevator shaft. At the other end of the cable is a weight, which balances the combined weight of the elevator car and its passengers. Both the car and the weight are guided up and down by rails. An electric motor turns the pulley to raise or lower the car.

Safety is very important to elevator designers. A device called a governor operates the brakes if the elevator moves too quickly. If the cable breaks, the elevator will come to a halt. Even if the brakes do not work, the elevator will be halted safely by shock absorbers at the bottom of the shaft.

Above: Many modern elevators have built-in weight sensors. If these detect that there are too many people in the elevator, the car will not move. If a car is fully loaded it will not stop to pick up more passengers. Computers control the car, telling it which floors to stop at. The computer ensures that passengers have to wait the shortest time possible for an elevator.

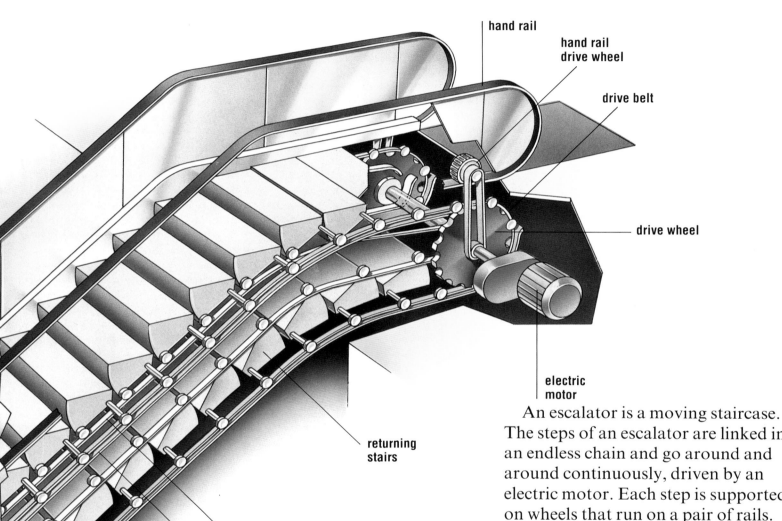

hand rail

hand rail
drive wheel

drive belt

drive wheel

electric
motor

returning
stairs

inner rail

outer rail

wheel

Above: The escalator is the most efficient means of moving people from one floor to another. A single escalator can move 10,000 people in an hour.

An escalator is a moving staircase. The steps of an escalator are linked in an endless chain and go around and around continuously, driven by an electric motor. Each step is supported on wheels that run on a pair of rails. On the sloping part of the escalator, the rails are side by side, and the steps form a staircase. At the top and bottom, one of the rails goes under the other. This lowers the steps to form a flat surface, so that people can walk off and onto the escalator. The motor moving the escalator also moves a handrail for people to hold. A variation of the escalator, called a travelator, or moving sidewalk, is used to carry people around places such as airports. This is a continuous horizontal rubber belt which moves while people stand on it.

THE PHOTOCOPIER

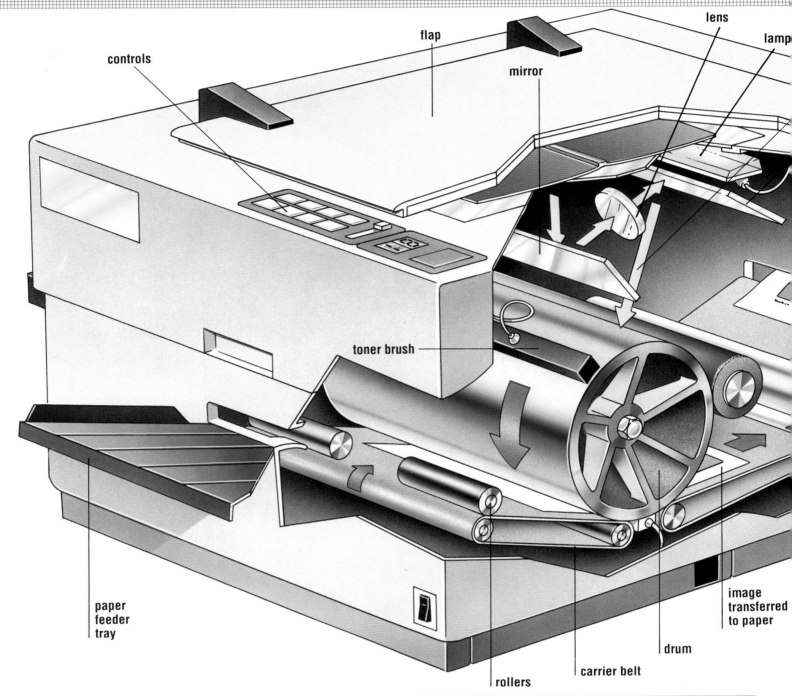

controls

flap

mirror

lens

lamp

toner brush

paper
feeder
tray

rollers

carrier belt

drum

image
transferred
to paper

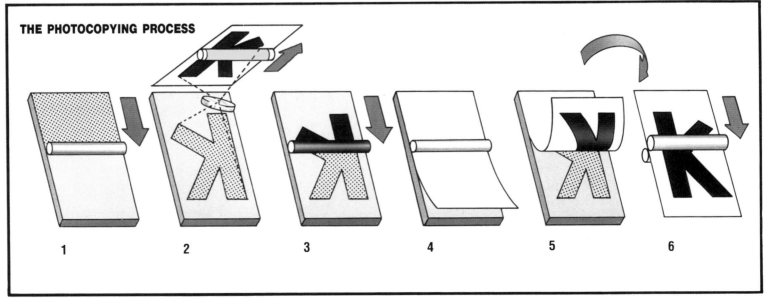

THE PHOTOCOPYING PROCESS

1   2   3   4   5   6

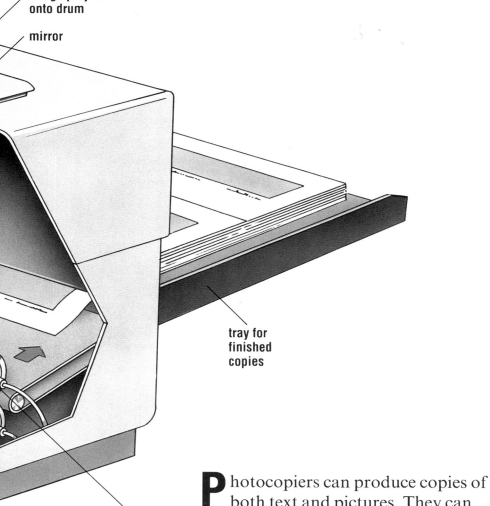

image projected onto drum

mirror

tray for finished copies

heated rollers

Left: The photocopying process.
1. The metal plate or cylinder is given an electric charge.
2. The image is focused on the plate by a lens.
3. Toning powder is brushed over the plate, sticking to the image.
4. Paper is pressed onto the plate.
5. Toner powder sticks to the paper.
6. The image is made permanent by heated rollers.

Photocopiers can produce copies of both text and pictures. They can make copies larger or smaller than the original. Some can even make colored copies of photographs or drawings.

The most modern type of photocopier uses a process called "xerography," a term derived from two Greek words meaning "dry writing." The process was invented in 1938 by Chester Carlson.

Inside a photocopier is a metal drum coated with a material, such as selenium, that can hold an electric charge when there is no light falling on it. The drum is given an electric charge before the copying process begins. To make a copy of a paper, a bright light inside the photocopier shines on it. Lenses (curved pieces of glass) direct the light from the paper onto the metal drum, forming an image of the paper on it. Where light strikes the metal surface, the electric charge leaks away through the selenium coating. Where the image is dark, the electric charge remains.

The drum is then dusted with a powder called a toner, which clings to the places where there is an electric charge. A sheet of paper is then wrapped around the drum and the toner transfers to the paper. The final step is to heat the paper briefly by running it between hot rollers. This melts the toner and makes it stick to the paper.

A cheaper type of photocopier, called an electrostatic copier, works in a similar way. The image is shone onto a special paper which holds an electric charge in the dark parts of the image. The paper is then coated with toner, which clings to the charged parts. The paper is then heated to fix the toner to it, producing a copy of the image.

THE TELEPHONE

The first telephone call was made on March 10, 1876. Into it, the inventor of the telephone, Alexander Graham Bell, spoke to his assistant, who was in another room. He said, "Mr Watson, please come here. I want you."

Although the telephone has been greatly improved since Bell's day, the principle remains the same. The mouthpiece contains a carbon microphone which has a metal diaphragm (thin sheet) at the front. Behind the diaphragm are loosely-packed carbon grains. When you speak into the mouthpiece, you make the diaphragm vibrate in time with the sound waves in your voice. The vibrations of the diaphragm cause the carbon grains to vibrate also, making the electric current flowing through the mouthpiece vary in time with the sound waves.

The electrical signal produced by the mouthpiece is mixed with another signal, called a carrier wave, before it is sent along the telephone line. This is done because the carrier wave is a rapidly changing signal that can travel more easily along the cable. At the receiving end of the telephone line, the electrical signal that is carrying the message is separated from the carrier wave. It is then amplified (made stronger) and sent to the earpiece.

The earpiece of a telephone contains a small loudspeaker that converts the electrical signals into sound. First, the signals pass through a coil of wire which acts like an electromagnet, causing a metal diaphragm to vibrate. The movements of the diaphragm cause the air to vibrate and the listener hears the vibrations as sound.

THE TELEPHONE EXCHANGE

local exchange

local exchange

main exchange

main exchange

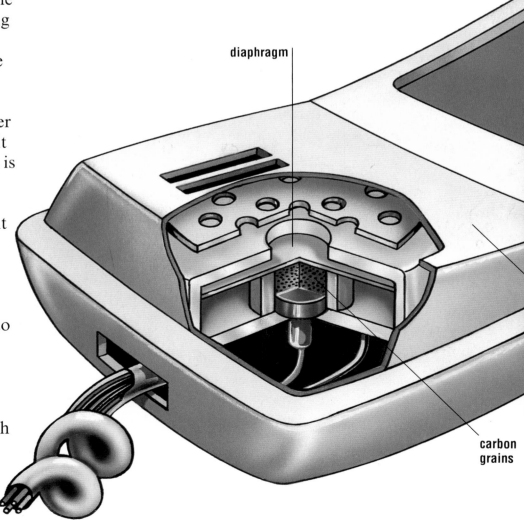

diaphragm

carbon grains

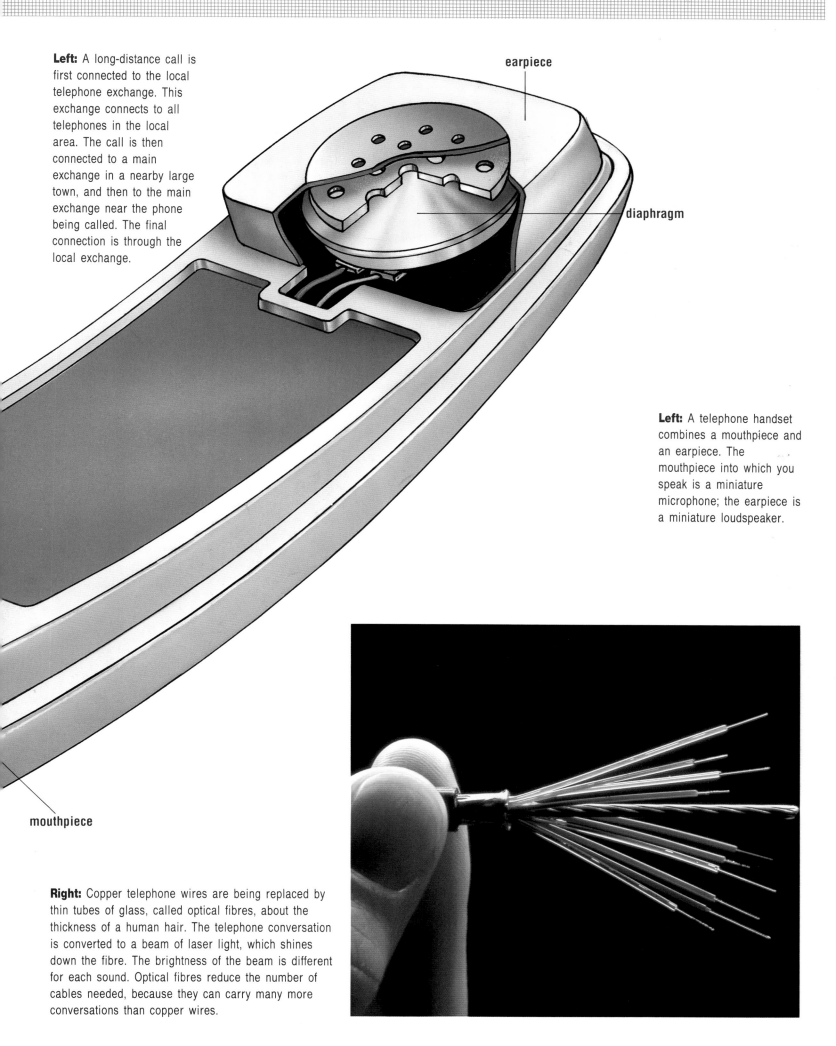

earpiece

diaphragm

Left: A long-distance call is first connected to the local telephone exchange. This exchange connects to all telephones in the local area. The call is then connected to a main exchange in a nearby large town, and then to the main exchange near the phone being called. The final connection is through the local exchange.

Left: A telephone handset combines a mouthpiece and an earpiece. The mouthpiece into which you speak is a miniature microphone; the earpiece is a miniature loudspeaker.

mouthpiece

Right: Copper telephone wires are being replaced by thin tubes of glass, called optical fibres, about the thickness of a human hair. The telephone conversation is converted to a beam of laser light, which shines down the fibre. The brightness of the beam is different for each sound. Optical fibres reduce the number of cables needed, because they can carry many more conversations than copper wires.

THE COMPUTER

Below: The output unit, called a monitor, is like a television set, except that it cannot pick up television programs. Some computers use home television sets as monitors.

Below: The microprocessor is the heart of a computer. It, and other silicon chips, are contained in the main computer box or unit.

Below: Floppy discs look like small bendy music records. They are inserted into the drive unit to read or write information.

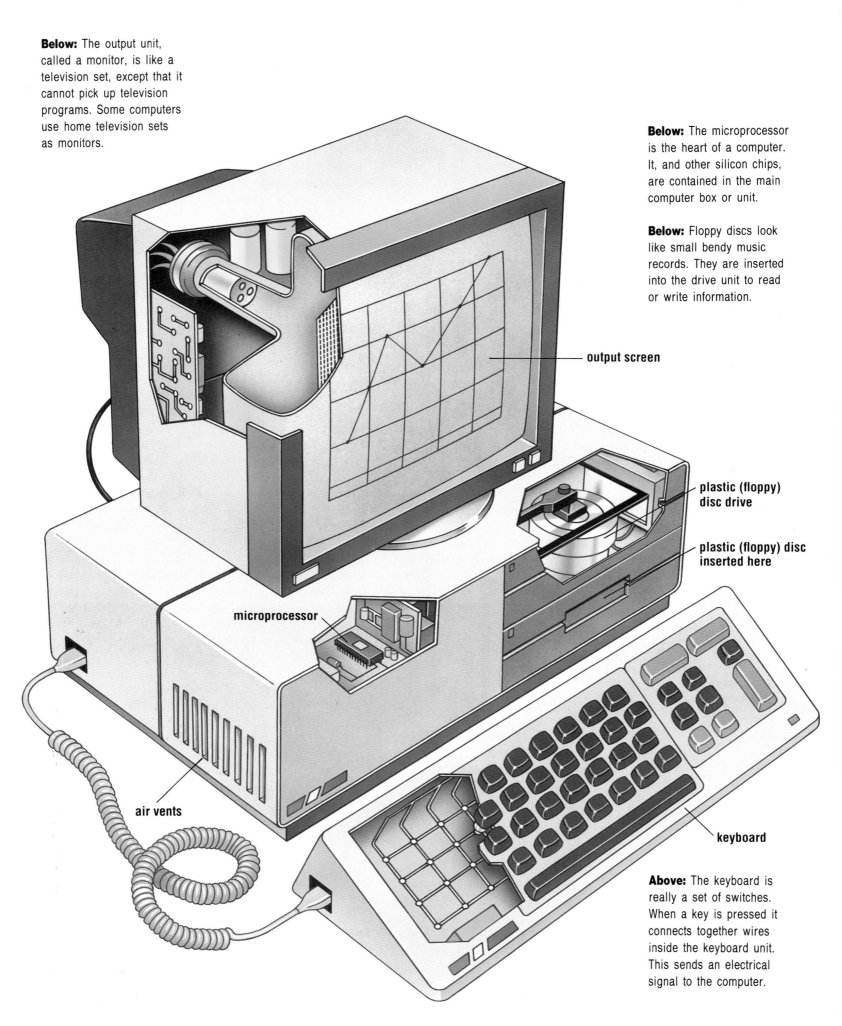

output screen

plastic (floppy) disc drive

plastic (floppy) disc inserted here

microprocessor

air vents

keyboard

Above: The keyboard is really a set of switches. When a key is pressed it connects together wires inside the keyboard unit. This sends an electrical signal to the computer.

The computer has been called an "electronic brain." The reason for this idea is clear. Computers can calculate and remember facts. Yet a computer is not a brain. It is merely an electronic device that can perform calculations at great speed.

There are four main parts to a computer. First there is an input device. This is often a keyboard like that on a typewriter. The keyboard is used to give information and instructions to the computer. Secondly, there is an output device. This is often a screen like that on a television. It shows the results of the computer's work. Thirdly, there is the computer's memory. One type of memory is called a floppy disc memory. This uses a plastic disc, like a small record, to hold information. The disc is inserted into a slot at the front of the computer when the computer needs the information held on the disc. There is additional memory inside the computer, in the form of silicon chips. These are small pieces of silicon – about the size of a child's fingernail – on which complete electronic circuits are built.

The fourth important part of a computer is a chip called a microprocessor. This does all the calculations and controls the operation of the computer. The microprocessor receives the list of instructions – the program – which is typed on the input keyboard. This has to be typed in using a simple language that the computer can understand. The microprocessor then does the calculations involved, calling on the memory for any information it needs. Finally, the microprocessor tells the screen to display the answers to the questions is has been set.

Right: Silicon chips, also called integrated circuits, are the building blocks of modern electronics. Each integrated circuit contains a complete electronic circuit on a small chip of silicon. The chip is contained in a package that makes it easier to handle, and is connected to the legs or pins by gold wires. There are many types of chip, each with a different job to do.

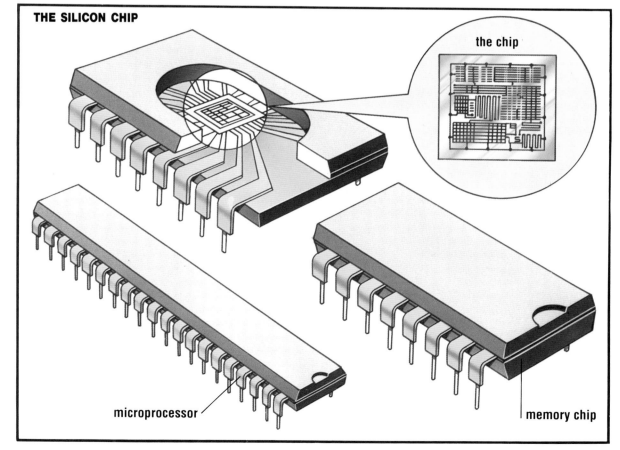

THE SILICON CHIP

the chip

microprocessor

memory chip

41

PAPERMAKING

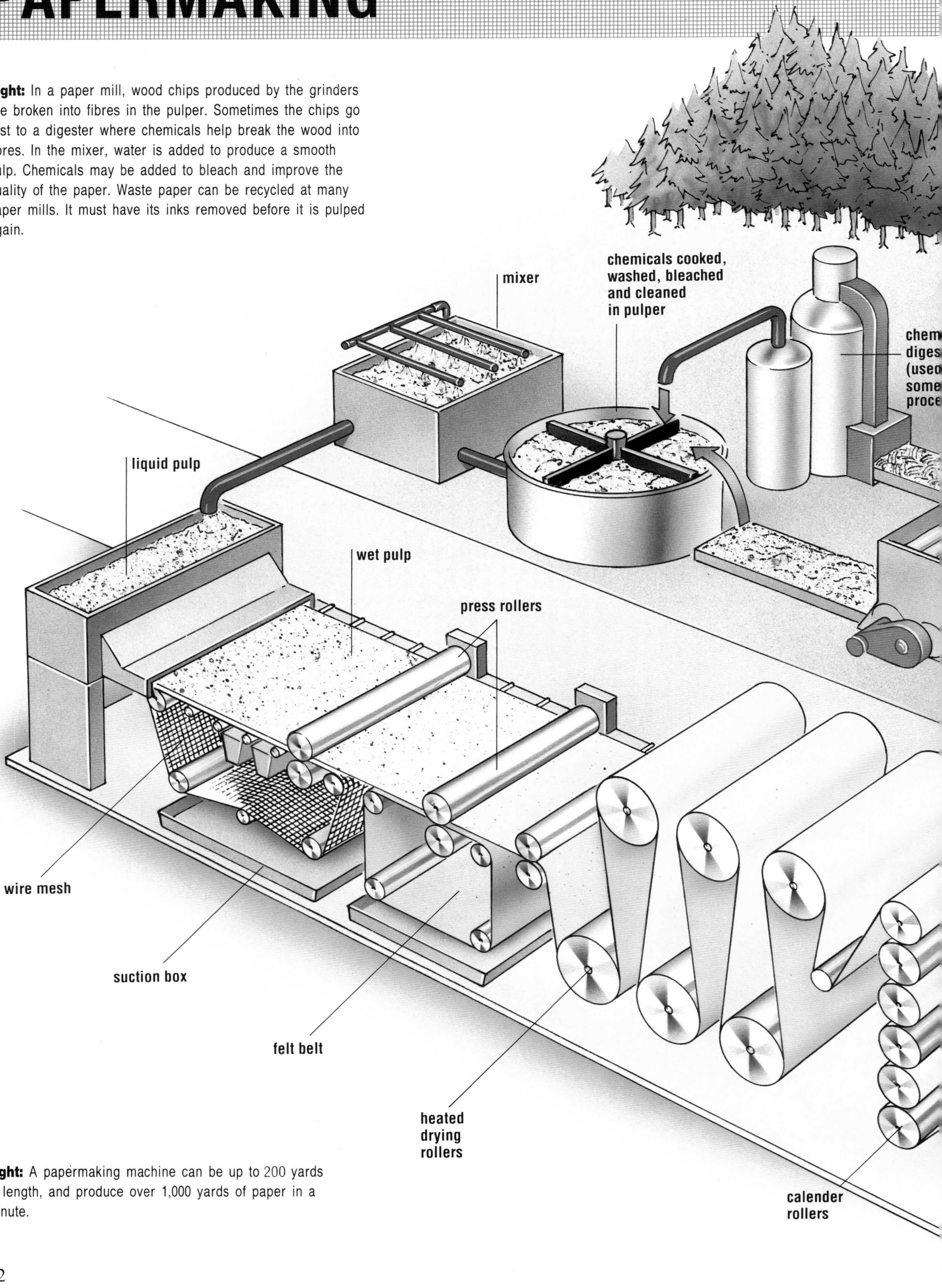

Right: In a paper mill, wood chips produced by the grinders are broken into fibres in the pulper. Sometimes the chips go first to a digester where chemicals help break the wood into fibres. In the mixer, water is added to produce a smooth pulp. Chemicals may be added to bleach and improve the quality of the paper. Waste paper can be recycled at many paper mills. It must have its inks removed before it is pulped again.

mixer

chemicals cooked, washed, bleached and cleaned in pulper

chem digest (used some proce

liquid pulp

wet pulp

press rollers

wire mesh

suction box

felt belt

heated drying rollers

calender rollers

Right: A papermaking machine can be up to 200 yards in length, and produce over 1,000 yards of paper in a minute.

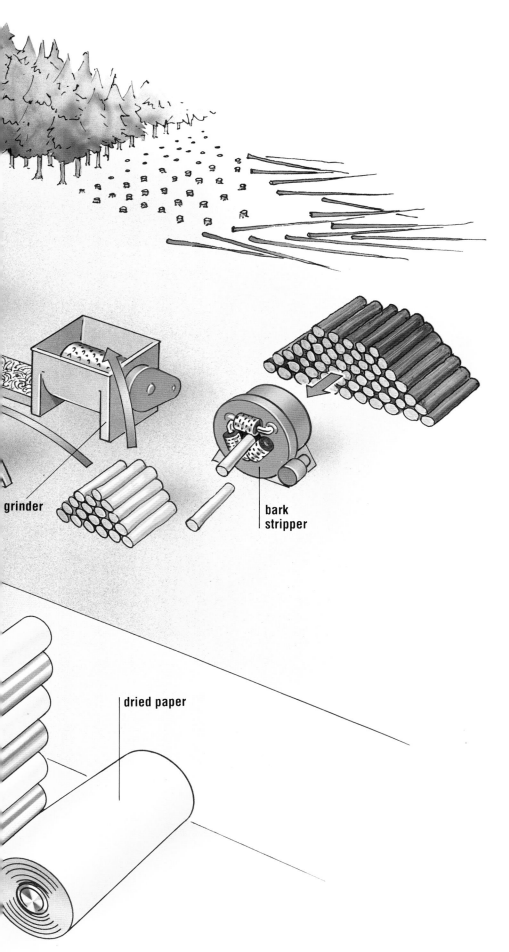

grinder

bark
stripper

dried paper

About 2,000 years ago, the Chinese first made paper by collecting together old fish nets, rags, and bits of plants. They boiled these with water, then beat them and stirred them to make a wet, soft pulp. A mesh made of fine criss-crossed wires was dipped into the pulp and then removed with a layer of pulp on it. After the water had drained away, the layer of pulp was pressed and dried to make paper.

Today, machines over 200 yards long are used to make paper. The process is basically the same as that used by the Chinese, but the raw material used is wood, from trees such as pine and spruce. One ton of paper can be made from 12 trees. The trees are first stripped of their bark, then ground to a pulp by giant stone grinders. The pulp is cooked with chemicals to break it into fibers, then washed, bleached and beaten into smaller, finer fibers. Finally, it is mixed with water.

Following these preparatory stages, the pulp is fed into one end of a long papermaking machine. The machine is called a Fourdrinier, after the two English brothers Henry and Sealy Fourdrinier, who developed it in 1803. The wet pulp is spread on an endless belt called a cloth, which is made of a wire or plastic mesh. Some water drains from the pulp through the mesh. More water is sucked out of the pulp by "suckers" below the mesh. The wet pulp is then transferred to a moving belt made of felt, where more water is squeezed out. Then it is fed onto large steam-heated cylinders which dry it. Finally, the paper passes through several rollers, which are highly polished and smooth the surface of the paper. The paper is then rolled onto a reel, or cut into sheets.

THE PRINTING PRESS

Johann Gutenberg, a German goldsmith, invented printing using movable type in 1450. First, individual letters were carved onto small blocks. The backgrounds were cut away so that the shapes of the letters stood out. Next, the type (the carved letters) was wiped with ink and pressed onto paper using a simple mechanical device, thus printing the letters. This process is called letterpress printing. It is still used, although two other processes are now much more common, namely lithography and gravure.

In lithography, the shape of a letter is produced photographically on a metal plate. The plate is treated with chemicals that make ink stick to the shape of the letter and not the plate. The plate is often wrapped around a cylinder which rotates at high speed. As it rotates, the plate presses against paper coming off a large reel. In a similar process called offset lithography, the inked plate first prints onto a rubber cylinder which then prints onto paper.

In gravure printing, the shape of the letters is etched by acids into the surface of a metal plate. Ink is trapped in the grooves formed on the plate and the plate is then pressed onto the paper, printing the letters. As with lithography, the plate is often curved around a cylinder to allow high-speed printing.

To produce a printing plate, typesetting machines with keyboards like typewriters first produce words on a photographic film. Light is then shone through the film onto a light-sensitive layer on the metal plate, transferring the image of the words to the plate. Illustrations can be added by using film of photographs or drawings.

Right: A newspaper printing press. This prints both sides of a continuous strip (called a web) of paper, four pages wide. Different colors are printed by using separate printing plates (called stereos). The machine cuts the web and folds the sections to make up the finished newspaper. When one reel of paper runs out, paper from another reel is automatically fed in, allowing the press to operate without stopping.

Below: In printing a full-color picture, four separate plates are made. One plate prints the cyan (blue) parts of the picture, the other plates print the magenta (red), yellow and black parts. The paper is passed over each plate in succession. The illustration shows how the picture builds up as each color is printed.

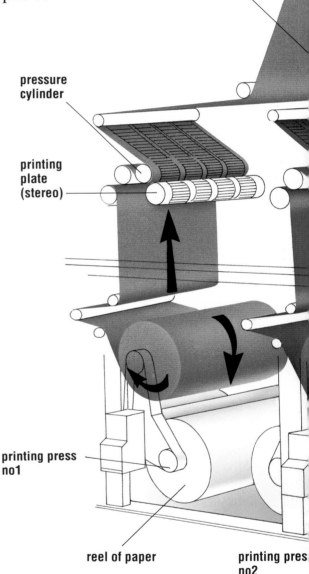

folding unit, to fold and combine different colour sections

pressure cylinder

printing plate (stereo)

printing press no1

reel of paper

printing press no2

THE COLOR PRINTING PROCESS

cyan (blue)

magenta (red)

yellow

black

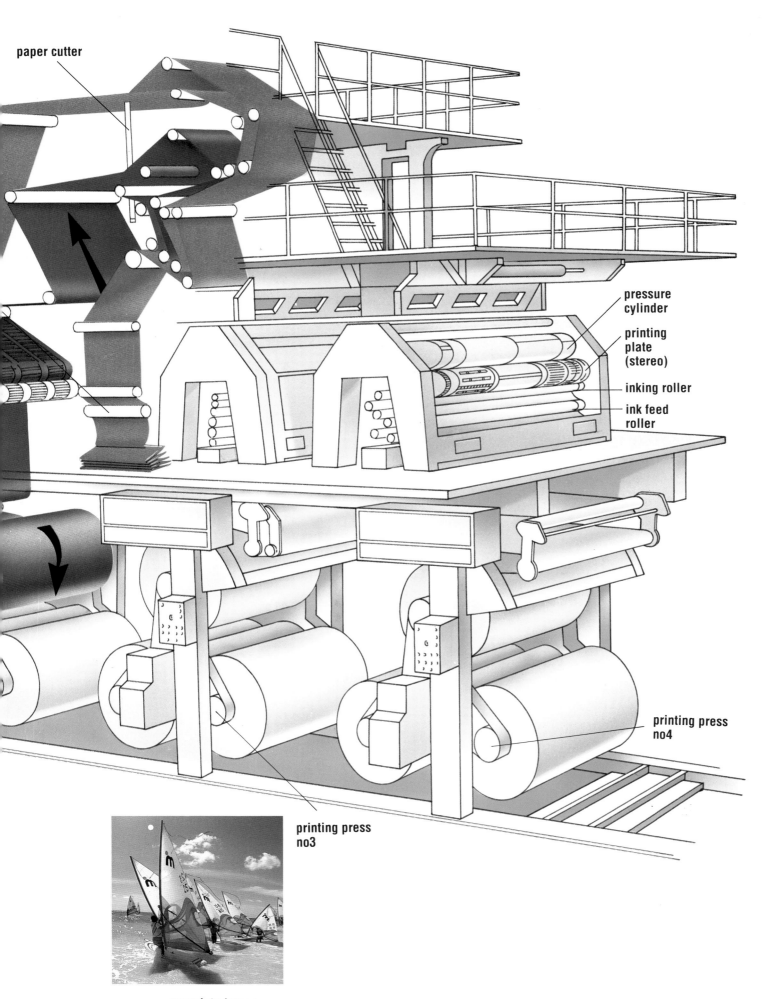

paper cutter

pressure cylinder

printing plate (stereo)

inking roller

ink feed roller

printing press no4

printing press no3

complete image

STEELMAKING

Steel is probably the most important of all metals. It is an alloy (mixture) of iron and small amounts of carbon.

The first stage in steelmaking is the production of iron in a blast furnace, a large upright cylinder about 50 yards high and 15 yards across. To do this, iron ore (a mineral consisting mainly of iron and oxygen), coke (a solid black material made by heating coal), and limestone (a common rock) are fed in at the top of the furnace.

Very hot air is blown into the furnace through holes called *tuyères* spaced around the bottom. Inside the furnace, the coke burns, melting the iron ore and producing a gas called carbon monoxide. The carbon monoxide combines with the oxygen in the iron ore, releasing the iron. The iron flows to the bottom of the furnace where it is drawn off.

The iron produced in a blast furnace is called pig iron. It is converted to steel by removing most of the carbon it contains. This is done in a converter which looks like a large steel bottle.

The first stage in the process is to pour molten iron into the top of the converter. Sometimes scrap iron is placed in the converter, too. Then a long pipe is lowered into the molten iron and a strong blast of oxygen is blown through the pipe. The oxygen burns away most of the carbon in the pig iron, producing steel. When the process is complete – it only takes about 30 minutes to produce 300 tons of steel – the converter is tipped on its side. The steel is then poured into molds, where it solidifies. Finally, it is rolled into flat sheets by heavy and powerful rollers.

Right: At a steelmaking plant, iron ore, coke and limestone are fed into the blast furnace. Heated air is blown into the furnace through the tuyères. Molten pig iron is extracted from the bottom of the furnace, and taken to the steel converter. Oxygen is blown into the converter, burning the carbon out of the iron and producing steel. The steel is poured from the converter and cast into blocks or ingots.

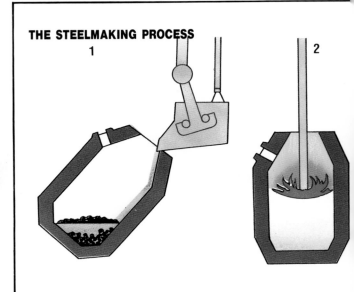

THE STEELMAKING PROCESS
1
2

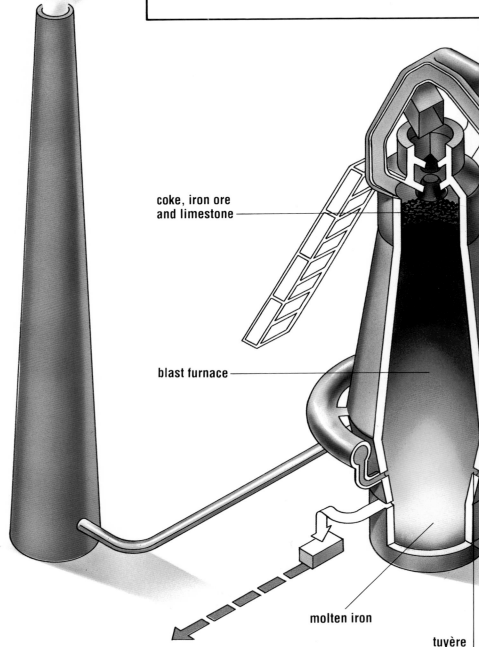

coke, iron ore and limestone

blast furnace

molten iron

tuyère

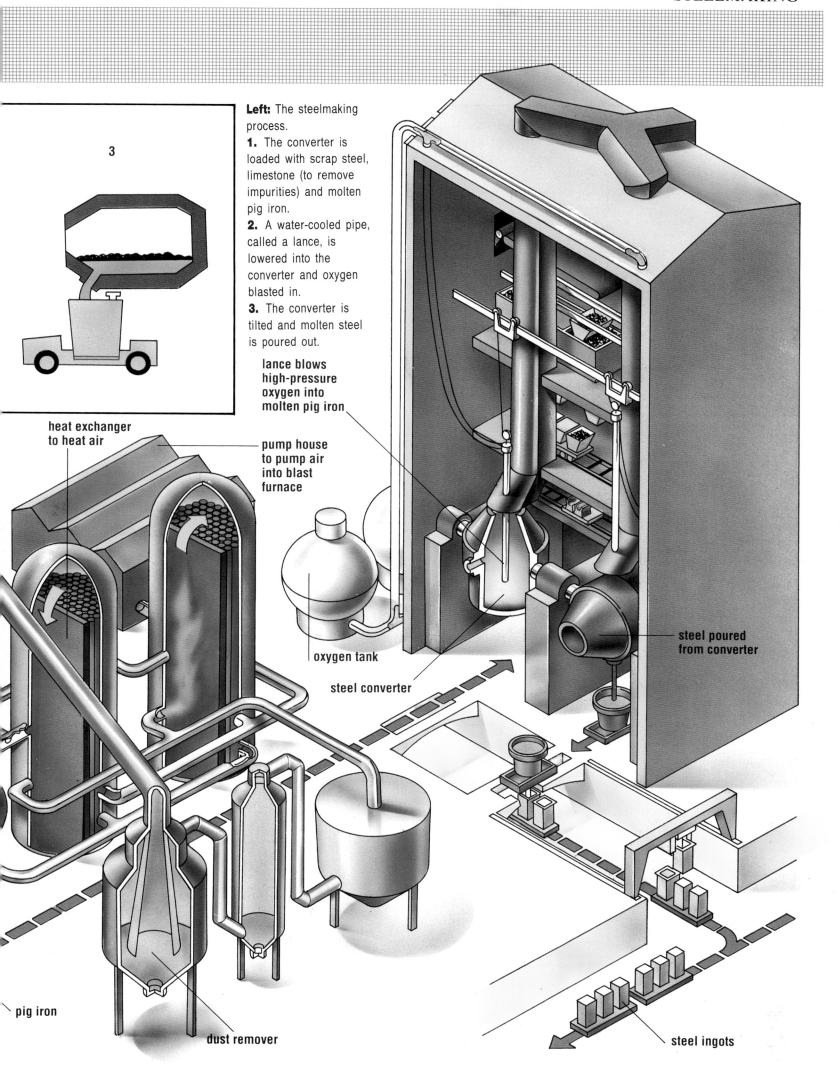

3

Left: The steelmaking process.
1. The converter is loaded with scrap steel, limestone (to remove impurities) and molten pig iron.
2. A water-cooled pipe, called a lance, is lowered into the converter and oxygen blasted in.
3. The converter is tilted and molten steel is poured out.

lance blows high-pressure oxygen into molten pig iron

heat exchanger to heat air

pump house to pump air into blast furnace

oxygen tank

steel converter

steel poured from converter

pig iron

dust remover

steel ingots

THE OIL-DRILLING RIG

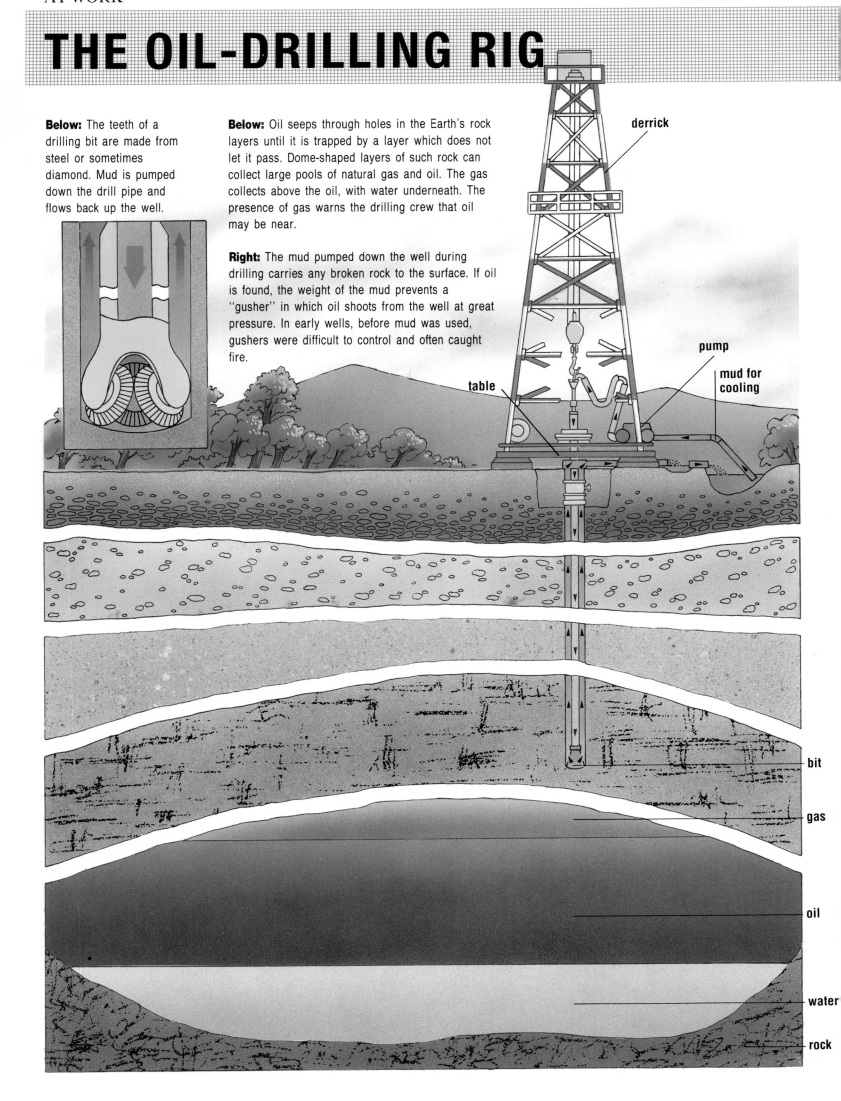

Below: The teeth of a drilling bit are made from steel or sometimes diamond. Mud is pumped down the drill pipe and flows back up the well.

Below: Oil seeps through holes in the Earth's rock layers until it is trapped by a layer which does not let it pass. Dome-shaped layers of such rock can collect large pools of natural gas and oil. The gas collects above the oil, with water underneath. The presence of gas warns the drilling crew that oil may be near.

Right: The mud pumped down the well during drilling carries any broken rock to the surface. If oil is found, the weight of the mud prevents a "gusher" in which oil shoots from the well at great pressure. In early wells, before mud was used, gushers were difficult to control and often caught fire.

derrick

pump

mud for cooling

table

bit

gas

oil

water

rock

The world's first oil well was drilled at Titusville, Pennsylvania, in August 1859 by Edwin L. Drake.

An oil well is drilled by a sharp bit which rotates to make the hole in the ground. The bit is like a dentist's drill, only much larger. It is connected to a "string" (lengths of pipe connected together) which turns as the hole is drilled. Above the well, looking like an electricity tower, is the derrick. This is used to lower the bit and pipes down the well.

The bit and string is turned by a rotating table at the base of the derrick. As the bit cuts into the ground, the pipe slides through the hole in the table. When the bit has descended to almost the end of the first section of pipe, drilling is stopped. Another length of pipe is then fitted to the top of the string and drilling starts up once more.

During drilling, special mud is pumped down inside the drill pipes. This mud cools and lubricates the bit, then flows up the well to the surface to be reused. The mud also helps strengthen the sides of the well, preventing a cave-in. However, stronger protection is given as soon as possible by lining the hole with a steel pipe called casing. Concrete is then poured between the casing and the wall of the hole.

A safety valve, called a blowout protector, is fitted to the top of the well while it is being drilled. If oil and mud is forced up the well by the pressure of the oil below, the valve can be closed. Later, after drilling has stopped, a valve called a "Christmas Tree" is fitted to the well. This allows oil to be drawn off in a steady stream.

Below: There are several different kinds of offshore drilling rig used to extract oil from under the sea. Semi-submersible rigs (left) float on the sea. They are anchored to the sea bed by cables. The Magnus rig (center) stands on huge steel legs. A production platform (right) is built above large tanks which sit on the sea bed. Oil from several wells is stored in the tanks until it can be taken ashore.

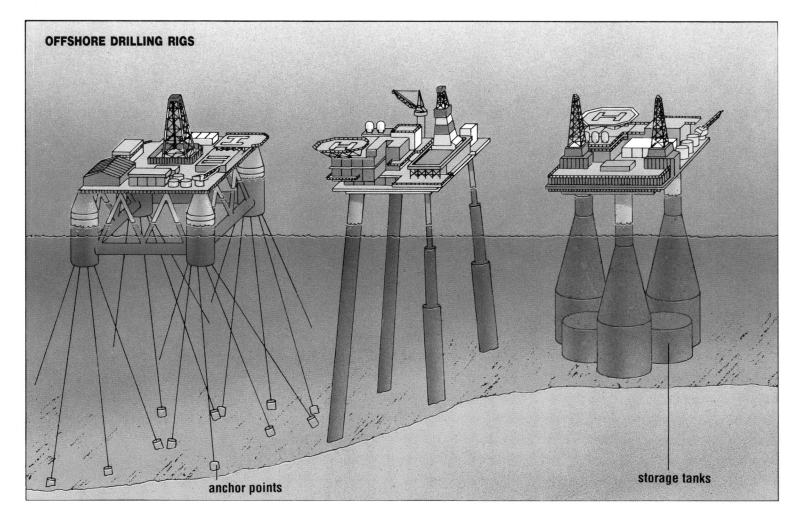

OFFSHORE DRILLING RIGS

anchor points

storage tanks

THE OIL REFINERY

Oil is valuable because so many useful substances can be made from it. Gasoline, lubricating oils, asphalt, diesel fuel, paraffin (kerosene), and wax all come from oil. In addition, many plastics, drugs, paints, explosives, and pesticides are made from substances originally processed from oil.

Crude oil which comes from an oil well is a black and thick liquid. It has to be refined – cleaned and changed into more useful substances – before it can be used. The first step in refining crude oil is to heat it, causing it to give off gases. This process is called distillation. The gases then pass into a tall column, called a distillation column. They flow up the column, passing through holes in trays set across the column, cooling as they travel upward. When the different gases have cooled sufficiently, they change into liquids. The liquids collect on a tray and are drawn off along pipes. Each pipe draws off a different liquid, called a fraction.

The lightest fraction is drawn off at the top, and the heaviest at the bottom of the column. Propane gas, useful as camping gas, is produced at the top of the column, asphalt at the bottom. In between, gasoline, paraffin, motor oil, and waxes are all produced.

Heavy fractions, such as wax, can be changed into more valuable light fractions. The process uses a chemical catalyst (substance which speeds up reactions) to crack (break) the heavy fractions. This process is called catalytic cracking. It is also possible to change light fractions into heavier ones. This process is called reforming. By using these processes, it is possible to make many different chemicals from the various fractions.

Right: Crude oil enters the system and, after mixing with the catalyst from the regenerator, goes to the reactor where some of the oil is broken into simpler substances. The vapor produced is then pumped to the distillation column where it is separated into petroleum gases, light and heavy oils, and a tar-like residue. The catalyst, mixed with steam and hot air, flows back to the regenerator, where it is cleaned for reuse.

waste gases

steam generator

crude oil

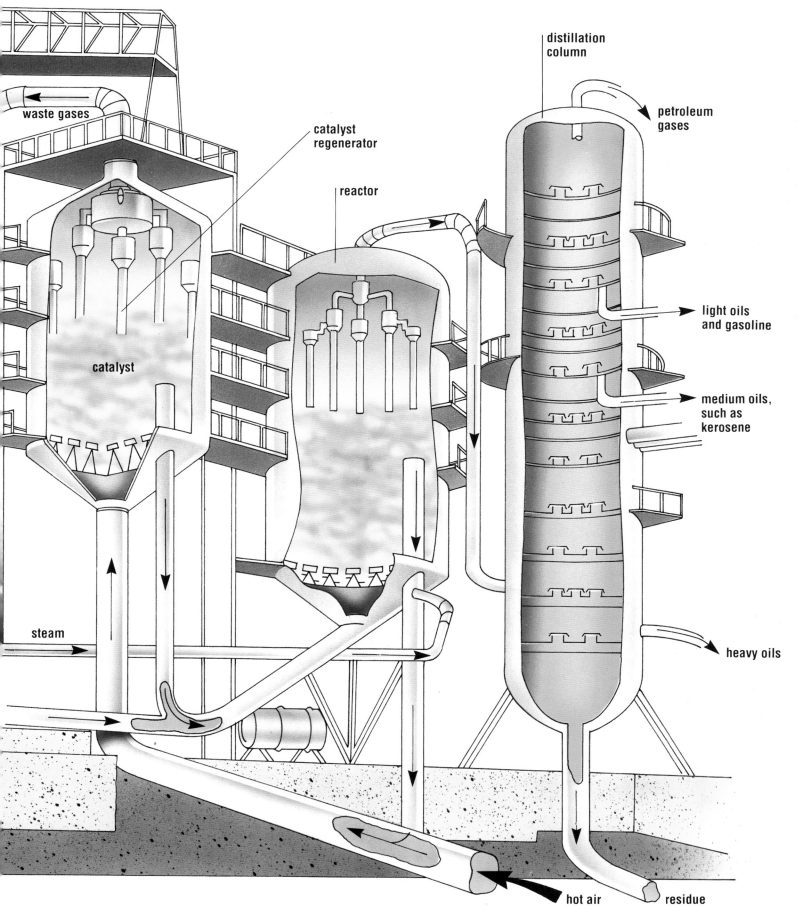

waste gases

catalyst
regenerator

reactor

distillation
column

petroleum
gases

light oils
and gasoline

catalyst

medium oils,
such as
kerosene

steam

heavy oils

hot air   residue

THE LASER

Below: A gas laser. The light produced by a laser is a single pure color. The light waves are all of exactly the same length, called the wavelength. Also, the waves are all in step with each other, which means the beam is very powerful.

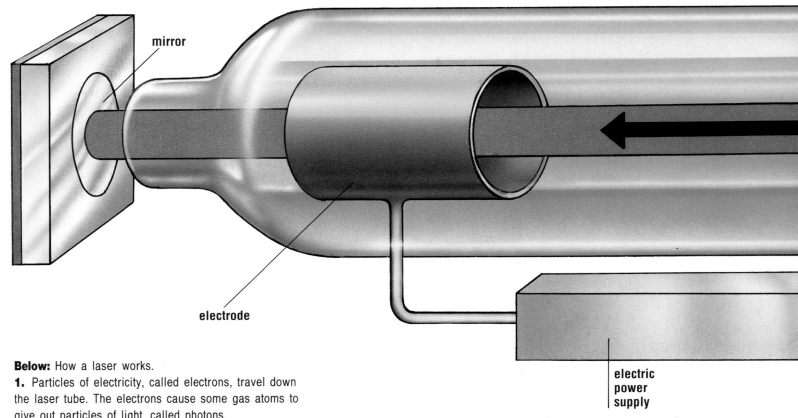

mirror

electrode

electric power supply

Below: How a laser works.

1. Particles of electricity, called electrons, travel down the laser tube. The electrons cause some gas atoms to give out particles of light, called photons.

2. A photon, passing an atom, causes it to give out another photon.

3. The photons pass backward and forward between the mirrors. The beam of light grows in strength as more and more atoms emit photons, until it is powerful enough to escape through the semi-transparent mirror.

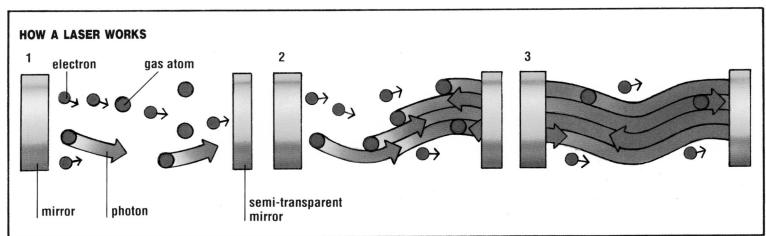

HOW A LASER WORKS

1   electron   gas atom   2   3

mirror   photon   semi-transparent mirror

Right: A laser light show demonstrates two properties of lasers: they produce a bright, narrow beam which does not spread out much, and the beam is a "pure" color.

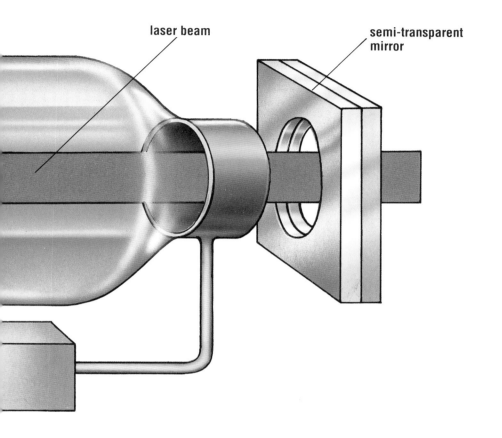

laser beam

semi-transparent mirror

A laser is a device that can produce a very powerful beam of light. The beam is very thin and does not spread out as it travels along. Lasers are used for tasks such as welding and eye surgery, and for disco lights.

The word laser is really a set of initials that stands for Light Amplification by Stimulated Emission of Radiation. This name was chosen because a laser stimulates its atoms to amplify (make stronger) a pulse or flash of light.

One type of laser, the gas laser, uses a small glass tube containing the gases helium and neon to produce its light. At each end of the glass tube is a mirror, one of which is semi-transparent so that a bright beam of light can pass through it.

Inside the tube are two metal electrodes. When the electrodes are connected to a supply of electricity, an electric current flows along the tube and the atoms of gas absorb energy from it. After a short time, however, one of the atoms can no longer hold the energy it has absorbed. This atom therefore releases a small pulse of light, called a photon, to carry the energy away. As the photon moves past the other atoms, it stimulates them to release their energy too. As a result they give off pulses of light as well. Because all the atoms release the pulses at the same time, a narrow, powerful beam of light is produced. The beam travels back and forth between the mirrors, gradually becoming brighter and brighter as more gas atoms are persuaded to release light. Eventually, the beam is bright enough to escape through the semi-transparent mirror.

THE BAR CODE READER

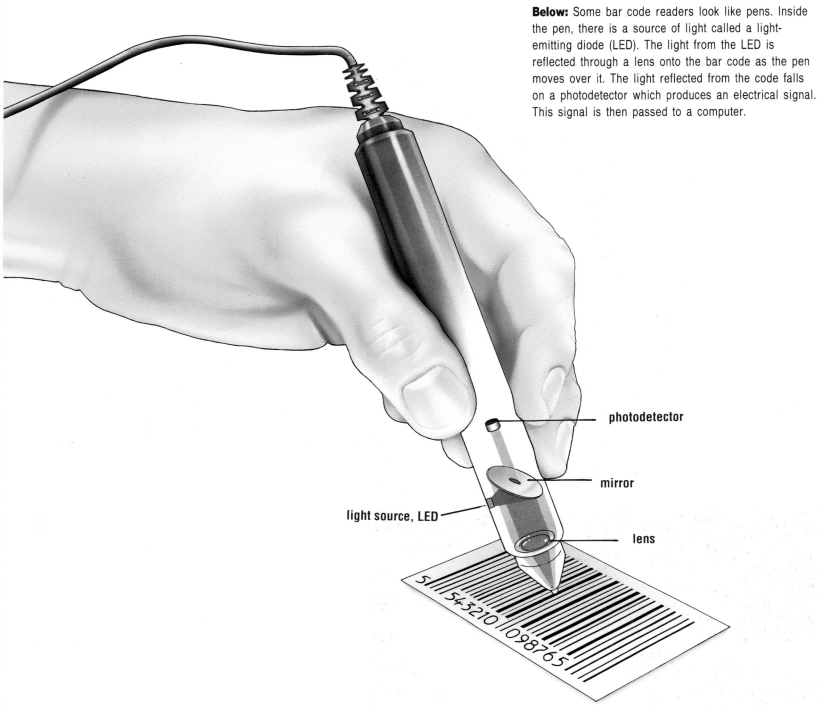

Below: Some bar code readers look like pens. Inside the pen, there is a source of light called a light-emitting diode (LED). The light from the LED is reflected through a lens onto the bar code as the pen moves over it. The light reflected from the code falls on a photodetector which produces an electrical signal. This signal is then passed to a computer.

photodetector

mirror

light source, LED

lens

5 543210 098765

A bar code is a rectangular block of black and white lines often seen printed on cans of food, books, and many other items. The dark lines and white spaces of different widths tell a computer what the item is and how much the item costs.

The information in the bar code is passed to a computer by a bar code reader. There are several different kinds of reader, but they all work in a similar way. First, a small beam of light is moved across the bar code. The dark lines in the code reflect less light than the white spaces, so the light reflected off the code varies in brightness. The reader converts the changes in brightness of the reflected light into an electrical signal. Finally, the signal is sent to a computer.

One kind of reader looks like a pistol. It is held in one hand and pointed at the bar code. Inside the reader is a laser which produces a

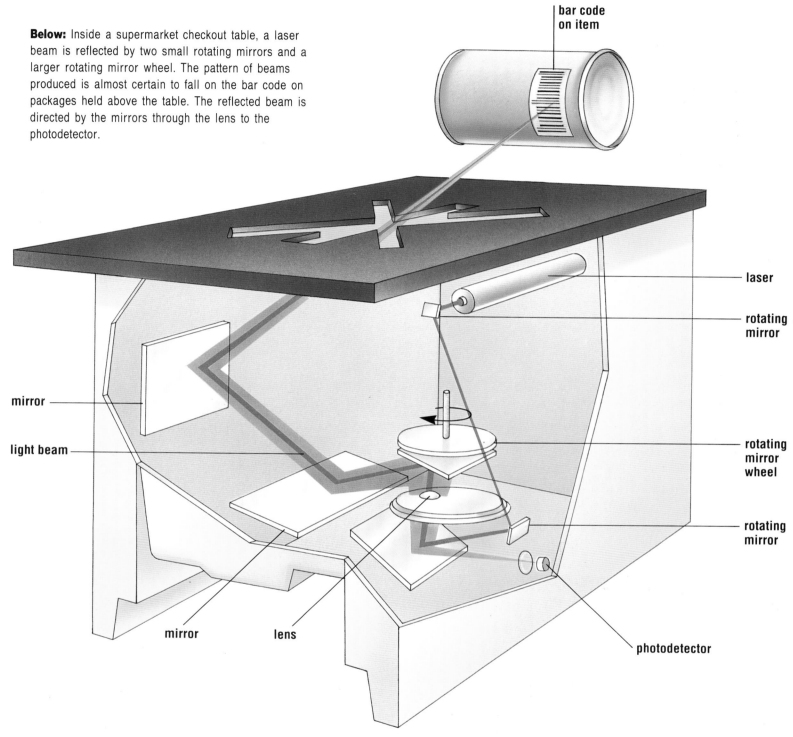

Below: Inside a supermarket checkout table, a laser beam is reflected by two small rotating mirrors and a larger rotating mirror wheel. The pattern of beams produced is almost certain to fall on the bar code on packages held above the table. The reflected beam is directed by the mirrors through the lens to the photodetector.

bar code
on item

laser

rotating
mirror

mirror

light beam

rotating
mirror
wheel

rotating
mirror

mirror   lens

photodetector

bright beam of light. The beam is bounced off a mirror which shakes back and forth inside the reader. As the mirror moves, the beam sweeps backward and forward across the bar code. Light reflected from the code travels back to the reader and falls on a detector, called a photodetector, which measures its brightness. The detector then produces an electrical signal for the computer.

A supermarket checkout works in the same way. A laser produces a beam of light which bounces off several moving mirrors. This produces a criss-cross pattern of light beams. When this pattern falls on an item of grocery, one beam of light is sure to fall across the bar code. Reflected light from the code is then directed by the mirror into a photodetector, which turns it into an electrical signal in the usual way.

THE X-RAY SCANNER

The invisible rays known as X-rays are very useful because they can pass through our bodies. An X-ray scanner uses them to produce a picture of the inside of a patient's body.

A scanner is a large machine with a hole in the center. The person being X-rayed (scanned) lies on a narrow table, which slowly moves into the hole. A narrow beam of X-rays is produced by a glass tube in which high-voltage electricity hits a metal target. The X-ray tube moves in a circle around the person being scanned. Sensitive detectors move around the person at the same time, keeping opposite the X-ray tube. The detectors are made of crystals that produce an electrical signal when X-rays fall on them. They are designed to measure how many X-rays are passing through the patient at any one time. After the X-ray tube has completed one circle, the patient is moved forward a little, and the process is repeated.

The signal produced by the detectors is fed to a computer. The computer holds information about the amount of X-rays absorbed by different types of body materials, such as fat, water, and bone. The computer compares the amount of X-rays being absorbed by the patient with the amount normally absorbed. It is able to build up a detailed picture of the inside of the patient's body. This picture is displayed on a screen for the doctor to examine. Each time the scanner moves around the patient, a picture is produced of a slice through the body. For this reason, these scanners are sometimes called computerized tomography (CT) scanners. (The word "tomography" comes from the Greek word *tomē* which means "slice".)

Below: A CT scanner is operated from a computer keyboard. The screens show the operator which part of the body is being scanned, and ensure that only a safe dose of X-rays is given. The picture of the patient's body produced by the scanner is also displayed on the screen.

THE X-RAY TUBE

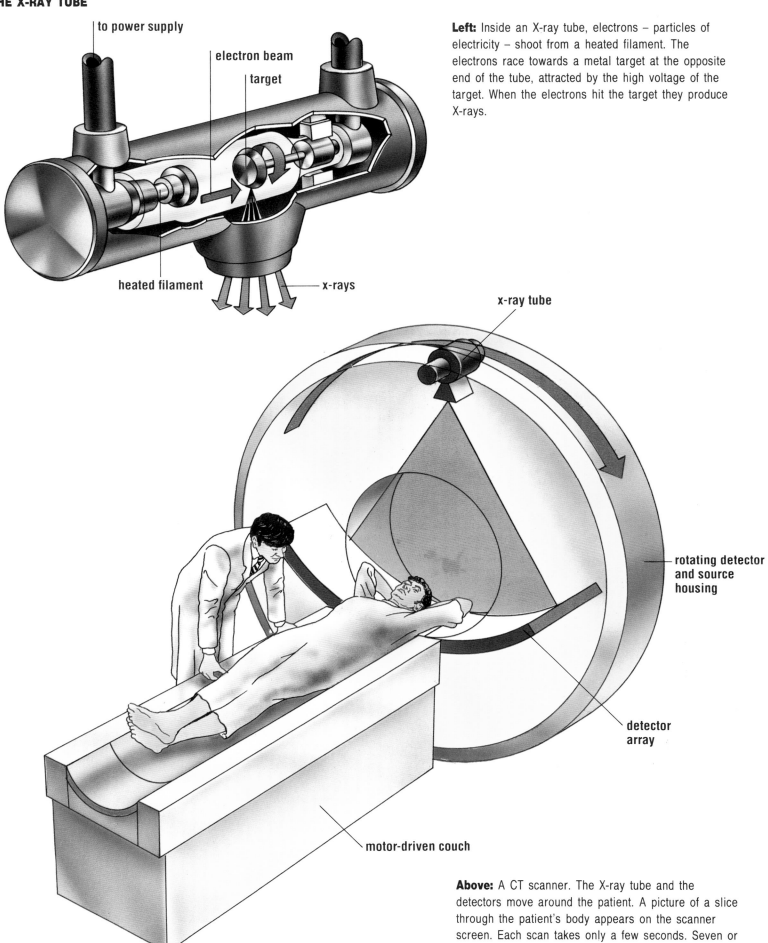

to power supply

electron beam

target

heated filament

x-rays

Left: Inside an X-ray tube, electrons – particles of electricity – shoot from a heated filament. The electrons race towards a metal target at the opposite end of the tube, attracted by the high voltage of the target. When the electrons hit the target they produce X-rays.

x-ray tube

rotating detector and source housing

detector array

motor-driven couch

Above: A CT scanner. The X-ray tube and the detectors move around the patient. A picture of a slice through the patient's body appears on the scanner screen. Each scan takes only a few seconds. Seven or eight slices might be scanned to examine a liver, for example.

THE DIALYSIS MACHINE

Below: A typical dialysis machine. Blood flows from the patient's artery to the artificial kidney where it is cleansed. It then flows back to the patient's vein.

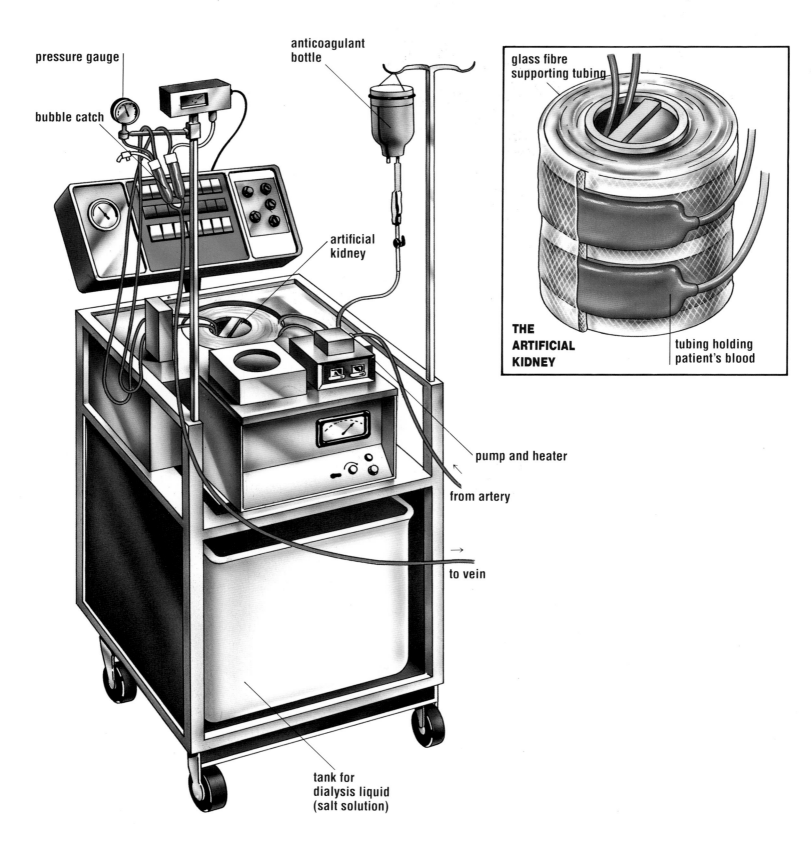

pressure gauge

bubble catch

anticoagulant bottle

glass fibre supporting tubing

artificial kidney

THE ARTIFICIAL KIDNEY

tubing holding patient's blood

pump and heater

from artery

to vein

tank for dialysis liquid (salt solution)

Above: The artificial kidney is a tube of thin plastic along which the patient's blood flows. The tube is wrapped in glass fibre and immersed in the dialysis liquid, a strong salt water solution.

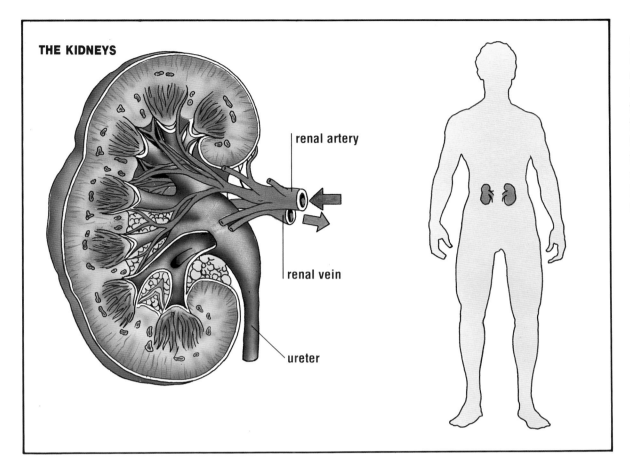

THE KIDNEYS

renal artery

renal vein

ureter

Left: Blood flows into our kidneys through a large artery, called the renal artery. After it is cleansed, the blood leaves the kidney through the renal vein. Waste chemicals taken from the blood are mixed with water to form urine. This leaves the kidney through the ureter.

Our two bean-shaped kidneys are found inside our body in the lower back area. They clean our blood, removing excess water and unwanted chemicals. People whose kidneys have stopped working must use a dialysis machine which is designed to clean their blood for them.

A person whose kidneys have failed is connected to a dialysis machine by two tubes. One tube is attached to an artery – a blood vessel that takes blood from the heart – in the patient's arm. Blood flows along this tube to the machine. After passing through the machine, the blood flows through the other tube back to a vein – a blood vessel that takes blood to the heart – in the same arm.

Inside the dialysis machine, the blood is cleaned. As a first step, medicines called anticoagulants are added to the blood to stop it from clotting as it goes through the machine. Then the blood is pumped through a long tube made of thin cellophane or plastic sheet called a membrane. The tube is surrounded by a strong salt water solution. Because the salt solution is so strong, water and waste chemicals from the blood pass through the membrane into it. The cleaned blood is then warmed up to body heat and sent back into the patient's arm. About 7 fluid ounces of blood flow through the dialysis machine each minute. After several hours of treatment, all the patient's blood, about 8 pints, is clean.

Two or three treatments are needed each week. While they are carried out, the patient lies in bed and may even sleep. Portable dialysis machines allow patients to go on vacation. Nevertheless, many patients choose instead to have a kidney transplant operation, in which they receive a new kidney.

LOCKS

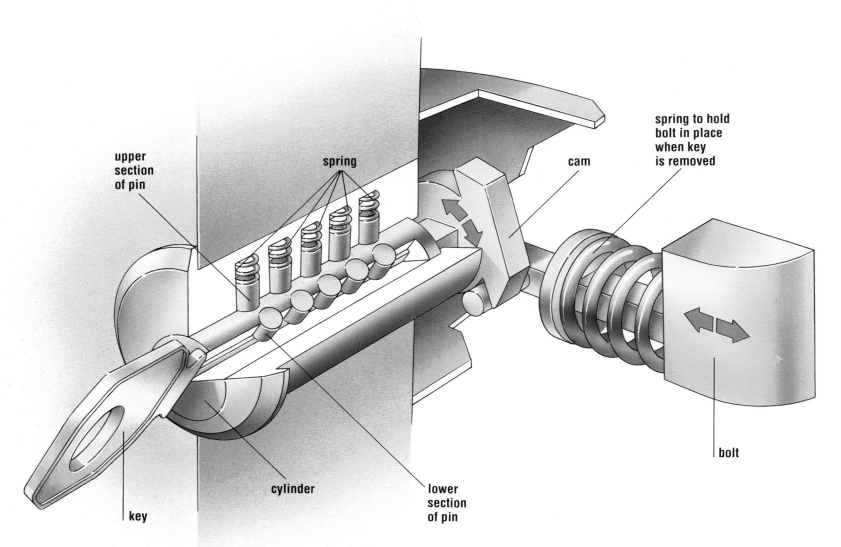

upper
section
of pin

spring

cam

spring to hold
bolt in place
when key
is removed

cylinder

lower
section
of pin

bolt

key

Above and Below: How a cylinder lock works.

1. When the key is inserted in the lock, it lifts each pin upward so that the cylinder can be turned. The cam attached to the cylinder pulls the bolt back.

2. When the key is removed, the small springs in the pin holes press the pins down, keeping the cylinder from moving.

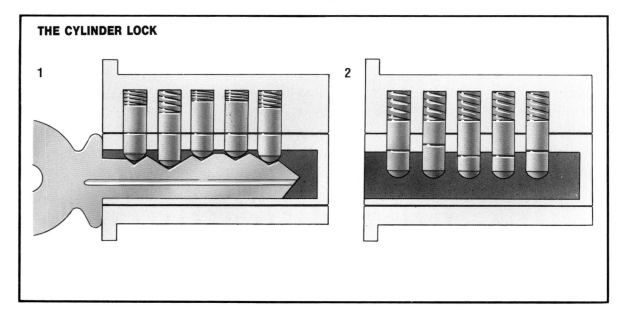

THE CYLINDER LOCK

1

2

Right: How a lever-tumbler lock works.

1. When the door is unlocked, the bolt is withdrawn from the door frame, held in place by the bolt pin in a slot at the back of the tumblers.

2. When the key is turned, the bolt pin slides along the slot in the tumblers.

3. When the door is locked, the bolt projects into the door frame, held in place by the bolt pin in a slot at the front of the tumblers.

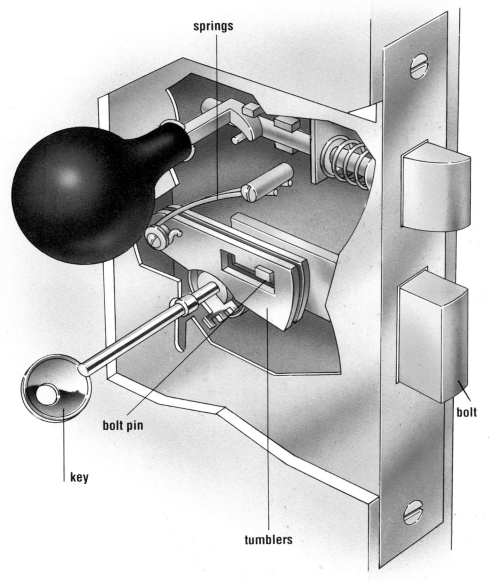

springs

key

bolt pin

tumblers

bolt

The earliest locks were made over 4,000 years ago by the Ancient Egyptians. Wooden locks have been found in the Pyramids in which a bar, called a bolt, moved out of the lock and fitted into the door frame. When the door was locked, the bar was held in position by pins which dropped from the door frame into the hollowed out bolt. To unlock the door, a simple key was inserted to push the pins upward so that the bolt could be moved.

Interestingly, the most common lock used to fasten the front doors of modern houses is very similar to the Egyptian version. It is called a cylinder lock. The modern version was invented in 1848 by Linus Yale, and as a result it is sometimes called a Yale lock.

In a cylinder lock, the key fits into a central cylinder connected to the bolt which prevents the door from opening. The cylinder is prevented from turning by five two-section metal pins which drop downward, pushed by springs, into the cylinder. When the correct key is inserted, the pins are lifted upward. The lower sections of the pins are lined up, allowing the cylinder to turn.

Another kind of lock is also used in modern houses. This is called the lever-tumbler lock. It was invented in 1778 by English locksmith Robert Barron. The most important part of the lever-tumbler lock is a lever that is held onto the bolt by a spring and prevents the bolt from moving. When the key is turned, it lifts the lever and moves it away from the bolt. The key is then able to move the bolt backward. Some locks have more than one lever and the key lifts each of them in turn.

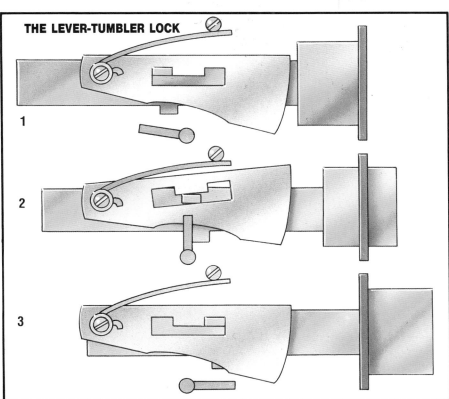

THE LEVER-TUMBLER LOCK

1

2

3

CLOCKS AND WATCHES

ALARM CLOCK
exploded view

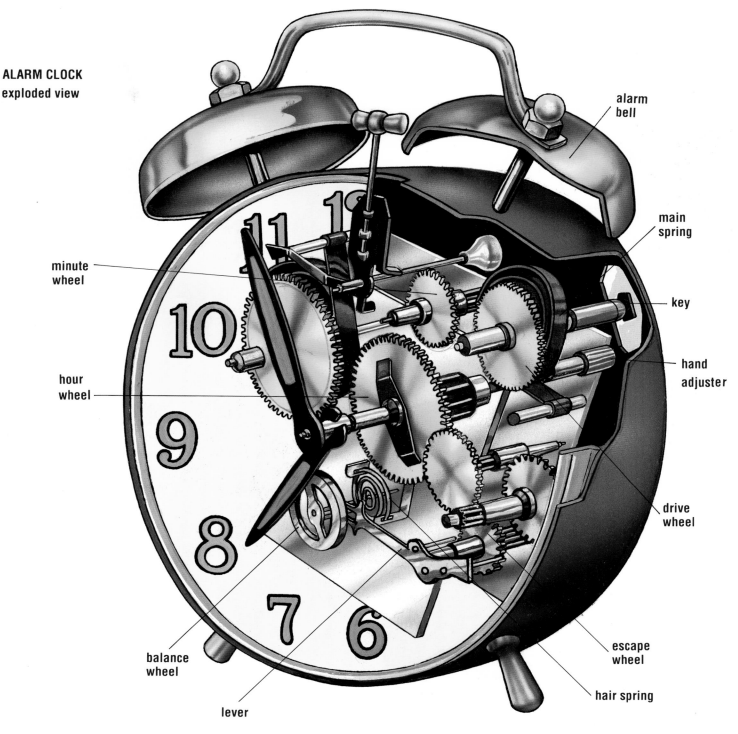

alarm bell

main spring

key

hand adjuster

minute wheel

hour wheel

drive wheel

escape wheel

hair spring

balance wheel

lever

Above: The many cogwheels inside a clock are used to connect the drive wheel (which turns the hands) with the balance wheel, which rotates backward and forward at a regular pace.

Clocks and watches look complicated. They are full of cogwheels and springs. However, they really have only two main parts. The first part, which turns the hands, is called the drive wheel. The second part, which makes sure that the hands are turned at a steady pace so that the clock keeps good time, is called the escapement. The cogwheels in a clock merely connect the drive wheel to the hands, and the

escapement to the drive wheel.

A type of clock seen in some houses is the grandfather clock. This clock uses a pendulum to ensure good timekeeping. The pendulum is a weight at the end of a metal rod. It swings back and forth, taking the same time for each swing, and rocks an "anchor" as it does so. The anchor keeps the drive wheel from moving, except for a short period during each swing. When the drive wheel is free to

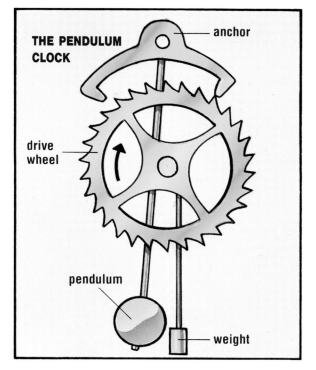

THE PENDULUM CLOCK

anchor

drive wheel

pendulum

weight

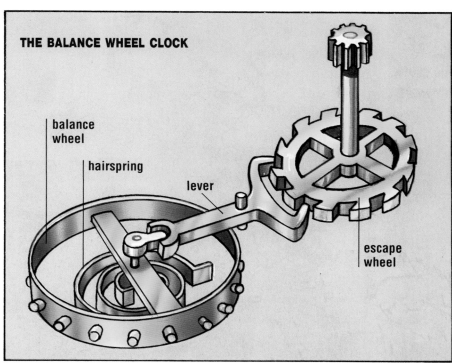

THE BALANCE WHEEL CLOCK

balance wheel

hairspring

lever

escape wheel

Above: In a pendulum clock, the swinging movement of the pendulum rocks the anchor backward and forward, allowing the drive wheel to move at regular intervals.

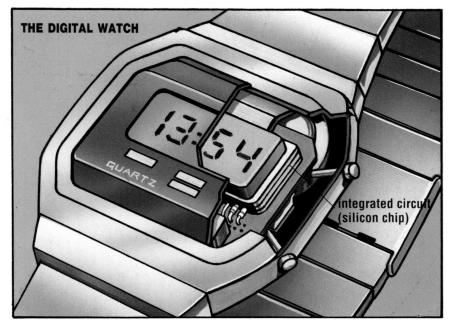

THE DIGITAL WATCH

QUARTZ

integrated circuit (silicon chip)

Above: In watches and small clocks, a balance wheel rotates backward and forward. This rocks the lever backward and forward, allowing the escape wheel to move.

Left: Inside a quartz digital watch, an integrated circuit, or silicon chip, counts the vibrations of a small quartz crystal. The vibrations are very precise and therefore a digital watch can keep time very accurately.

move, a weight connected to it falls. This turns the drive wheel and hands. Each time the anchor moves, it gives a tiny push to the pendulum in order to keep it swinging.

Smaller clocks and watches are often driven by a spring, called a mainspring, which is connected to the drive wheel. As the spring unwinds, it turns the drive wheel and hands. There is no pendulum in these clocks. Instead, a wheel, called a balance

wheel, moves back and forth, powered by a thin spring called a hairspring. The balance wheel is connected to a lever with teeth that fit into a cogged wheel, called an escape wheel. Each time the lever moves, it releases the escape wheel for a short length of time. This allows the mainspring to move the hands. Each time the escape wheel moves, it gives a push to the balance wheel to keep it moving, too.

HOUSEHOLD APPLIANCES

Electrical appliances are used for many tasks in the home. These appliances rely on the different effects of an electric current.

Many appliances, such as dishwashers, drills, vacuum cleaners, and razors, contain electric motors which use the magnetic effect of a current to produce motion. In a vacuum cleaner, for example, a small electric motor drives a fan which sucks air and dust into a bag. The bag removes the dust from the air, and the air is then blown out of the back of the cleaner. Upright cleaners have spiral brushes and beaters, driven by the motor, to stir up the dust. In a washing machine, the electric motor is used to pump water out, and to rotate the cylinder during washing and spin-drying.

In a refrigerator, an electric motor is used to pump a liquid, called a refrigerant, through pipes. The refrigerant is first compressed to a high pressure in one part of the refrigerator. At this high pressure, the refrigerant is a liquid. The compressed liquid is passed through a valve into a region of low pressure. As this happens, the liquid evaporates rapidly into a gas. This fast evaporation takes heat from the inside of the refrigerator. The refrigerant is then compressed again to turn it back into a liquid and reused.

Another effect of an electric current – the heating effect – is used in ovens, toasters, and fan heaters. In an electric iron, a wire called a heating filament glows red hot as electricity passes through it. This heats the metal surface of the iron. Ordinary electric light bulbs also rely on this effect. The filament of a light bulb becomes so hot that it glows brightly.

Below: In a refrigerator, a compressor pumps liquid – called a refrigerant – to the evaporator in the freezer compartment. The liquid changes to a vapor, absorbing heat and chilling the compartment. The vapor is then pumped to the condenser where it changes back to a liquid, giving up its heat to the outside air. The thermostat regulates the temperature by turning the compressor on when the temperature inside the fridge rises.

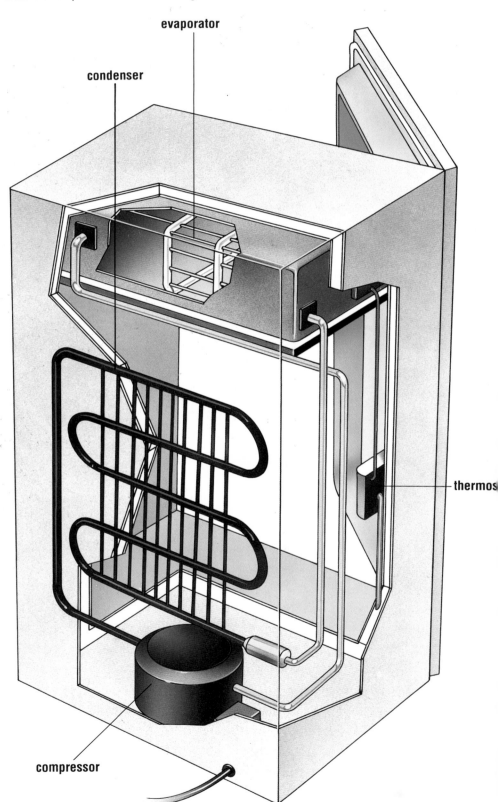

evaporator

condenser

thermos

compressor

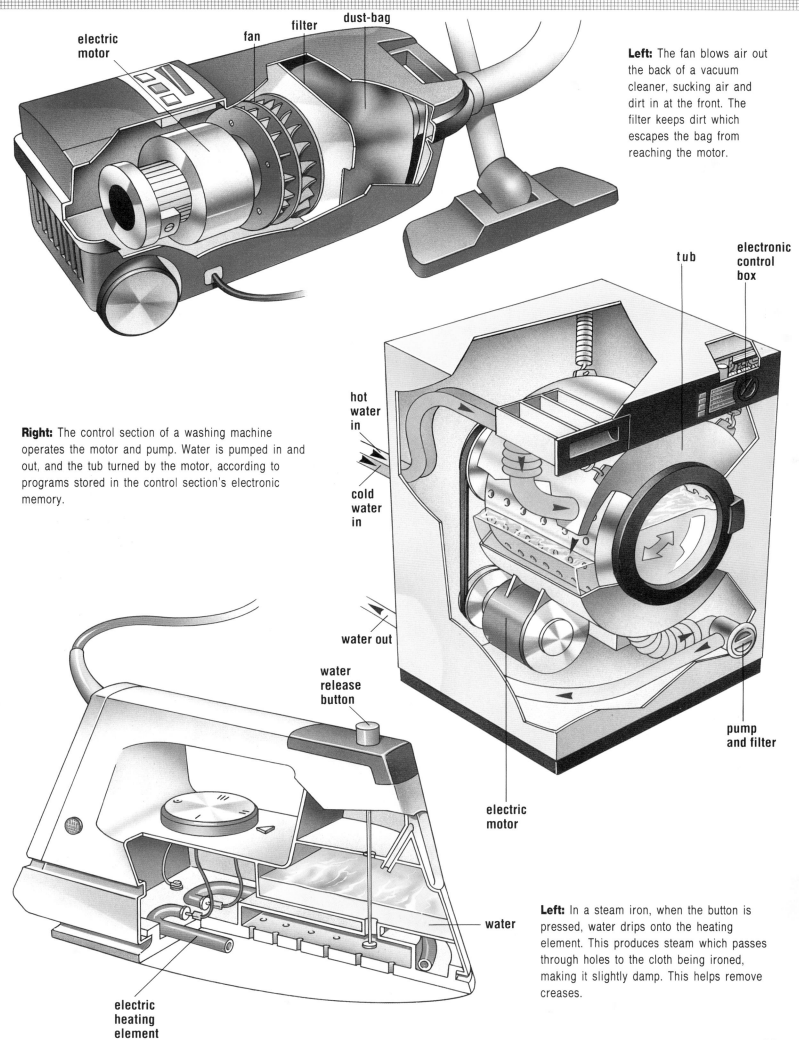

electric motor

fan

filter

dust-bag

Left: The fan blows air out the back of a vacuum cleaner, sucking air and dirt in at the front. The filter keeps dirt which escapes the bag from reaching the motor.

tub

electronic control box

Right: The control section of a washing machine operates the motor and pump. Water is pumped in and out, and the tub turned by the motor, according to programs stored in the control section's electronic memory.

hot water in

cold water in

water out

water release button

pump and filter

electric motor

electric heating element

water

Left: In a steam iron, when the button is pressed, water drips onto the heating element. This produces steam which passes through holes to the cloth being ironed, making it slightly damp. This helps remove creases.

THE RECORD PLAYER

Below: A hi-fi system produces sounds with "high-fidelity", which means they are very close to the original sounds that were recorded. These systems often have separate units to play records and tape cassettes. The amplifier is the heart of the system since it must strengthen the weak signals produced by the pick-up before they are fed to the loudspeakers. Most hi-fi systems are stereo and have two separate loudspeakers to produce more realistic sounds.

Below: The varying width of the groove in the record makes the stylus, or needle, vibrate as the record turns. In a stereo system with two loudspeakers, the movement of the needle to one side produces a signal which goes to one loudspeaker; the signal produced when the needle moves in the opposite direction goes to the other speaker.

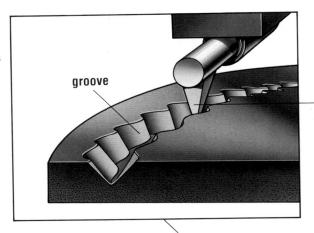

groove

stylus/needle

magnet

coil

Above: The pick-up turns the vibrations of the stylus, or needle, into an electrical signal. In a moving-coil pick-up, a coil of wire near a magnet is moved by the needle, and a signal flows in the coil.

Below: In a moving-coil loudspeaker, the amplified signals are fed to a coil of wire attached to the cone or diaphragm. This makes the cone vibrate, producing sound.

STEREO SOUND SYSTEM

record on turntable

tweeter

speaker

coil

circular magnet

woofer

cone or diaphragm

record player

compact disc player

radio

amplifier

cassette deck

In a record player, the record rests on a revolving table, called a turntable. A needle rests in the groove of the record. The needle is held in a device called a pick-up, at the end of a pick-up arm. As the record turns, the needle vibrates against the bumps in the groove. The tiny vibrations of the needle cause the pick-up to produce an electric current or signal which varies in step with the recorded music or words.

A commonly used kind of pick-up contains a special type of crystal, called a piezoelectric crystal. These crystals produce electricity when they are squeezed. As the needle bumps along the groove, its movements squeeze the crystal, producing an electric signal. Another kind of pick-up contains a tiny coil of wire near a strong magnet. The coil is attached to the needle. As the needle vibrates, the coil moves. This movement causes a small electric signal to be produced in it.

The signal produced by the pick-up is fed to an electronic circuit, called an amplifier. The amplifier strengthens the signal before sending it to the loudspeaker.

Inside a loudspeaker, there is a cone of thin cardboard or plastic called a diaphragm. The small end of the diaphragm is attached to a coil of wire near a permanent magnet. The signal from the amplifier flows through the coil. This turns the coil into an electromagnet, whose strength varies as the signal varies. The electromagnet moves as it is attracted and repelled by the permanent magnet. This causes the diaphragm to vibrate, producing the sounds we hear. Some loudspeakers have more than one cone. Large cones, called woofers, are used to produce low sounds. Small cones, called tweeters or squawkers, are used to produce high sounds.

Left: A compact disc (CD) is a disc with a metallic coating. The sound is represented by a series of pits cut in the disc. Instead of a needle touching the disc, a laser beam is used to read the pits. Compact discs are smaller and less easily damaged than normal records.

THE TAPE RECORDER

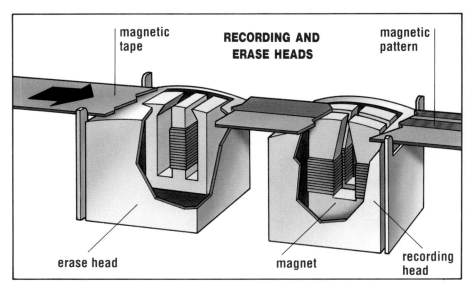

magnetic tape

RECORDING AND ERASE HEADS

magnetic pattern

erase head

magnet

recording head

Left: The recording head is a small electromagnet with a gap facing the tape. The varying electrical signals produced by the microphone passes through the coil of wire around the head, producing a varying pattern of magnetism on the tape. The erase head wipes the tape clean before it is recorded.

Below: The cassette tape recorder records on to tape contained in a lightweight box, or cassette. It is much easier to use a cassette than to thread the tape through the machine.

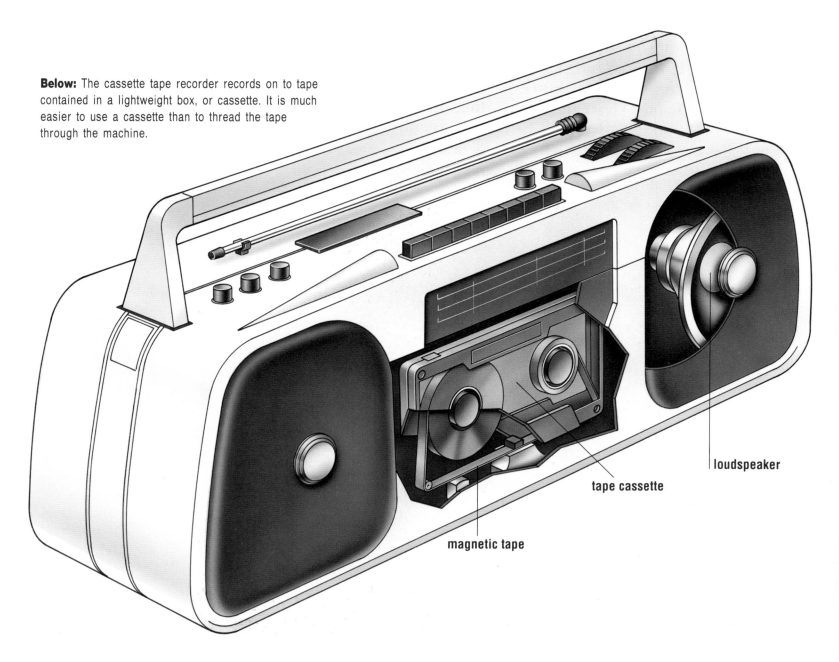

loudspeaker

tape cassette

magnetic tape

To produce a tape recording, sound is first converted into an electrical signal by a microphone. Inside the tape recorder, the signal is recorded as a magnetic pattern on a plastic tape.

The sounds falling on a microphone cause a diaphragm (thin plate) to vibrate. In a crystal microphone, the diaphragm is connected to a piezoelectric crystal. The vibrations of the diaphragm squeeze the crystal, producing an electrical current or signal which varies as the sounds vary.

The electrical signal is taken to the recording head in the recorder. This is a curved piece of iron with a coil of wire wound around it to make an electromagnet. The iron has a small gap between its ends, and as the signal flows through the coil, magnetism is produced in the gap. The tape, which has a thin coating of a magnetic material called iron oxide, is passed along close to the gap. As a result, the iron oxide is magnetized. The pattern of magnetism produced on the tape depends on the signal produced by the microphone. When the signal is strong, the tape is strongly magnetized accordingly.

To play back the recording, the tape is moved past a head, similar to the recording head, called a replay head. As the tape goes past the head, the magnetized parts of the tape cause a signal in the coil of the head. The stronger the magnetism on the tape, the stronger the signal produced. Thus the signal produced by the replay head is identical to the signal produced by the microphone during recording. The signal is then amplified and passed to the loudspeaker, where it is converted into sound.

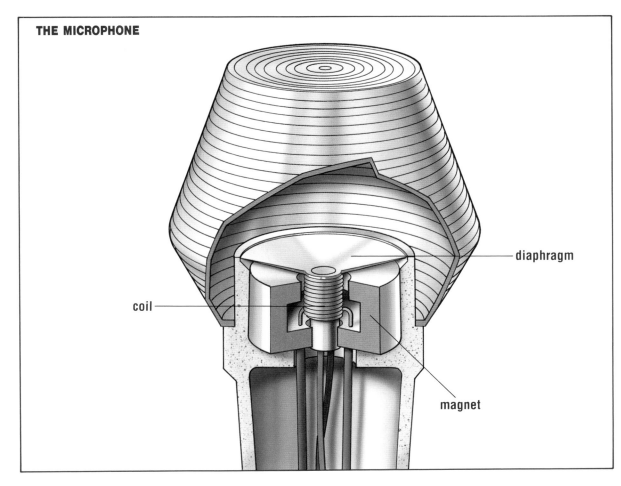

THE MICROPHONE

coil

diaphragm

magnet

Left: There are a number of different types of microphone. In this moving-coil microphone, sound waves striking the diaphragm make it vibrate. The coil attached to the diaphragm moves between the poles of the magnet. The movement causes the electric current through the coil to vary in time with the sound waves.

THE RADIO

Below: Most homes have a radio to receive radio programmes broadcast from radio stations. The tuning knob, or tuner, selects the signal from the required station.

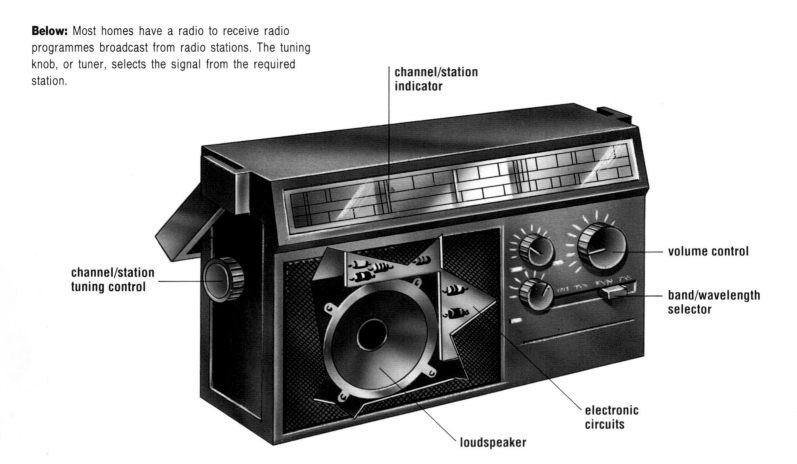

channel/station indicator

volume control

band/wavelength selector

channel/station tuning control

electronic circuits

loudspeaker

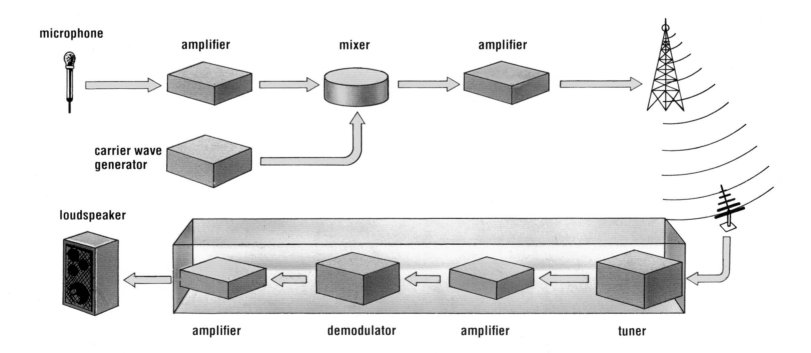

microphone

amplifier

mixer

amplifier

carrier wave generator

loudspeaker

amplifier

demodulator

amplifier

tuner

Above: At a radio transmitting station, the electrical signal produced by the microphone (the audio signal) is made stronger by the amplifier. Then it is mixed with the carrier wave. This process is called modulation. After another amplification, the signal is broadcast. In a radio receiver, the tuner selects the signal from the required station. The signal is then amplified and sent to the demodulator which separates the carrier and audio signals. The audio signal is amplified and sent to the loudspeaker.

R adio sets are often called receivers. This is because they receive a signal from a distant radio station. The station is called a transmitter because it transmits (sends out) the signal.

The signals sent out by the transmitter are called radio waves. This is because they spread out from the station in the same way as ripples or waves spread out across a pond after a pebble is dropped in it. They are in fact ripples of magnetism and electricity that can pass through empty space at a speed of about 187,000 miles per second. Another name for radio (and television) waves is electromagnetic waves.

At a radio station, radio waves are produced by an aerial or antenna, a metal wire high above the ground. A rapidly changing electric current is passed through the aerial, which causes the atoms in the aerial to vibrate, producing a radio wave called the carrier wave. The strength or frequency of the carrier wave is varied to carry the sounds. (The frequency is the number of waves produced each second.) This is done by connecting the studio microphone to the aerial, so that it modulates (alters) the carrier wave.

A radio receiver is also connected to an aerial or antenna. When a radio signal falls on the aerial, small electric currents start to flow in it. The signals from a particular radio station are selected by tuning the electronic circuits in the receiver. The electronic circuits then remove the carrier signal. The remaining sound signal is amplified and passed to the loudspeaker to be turned into sound.

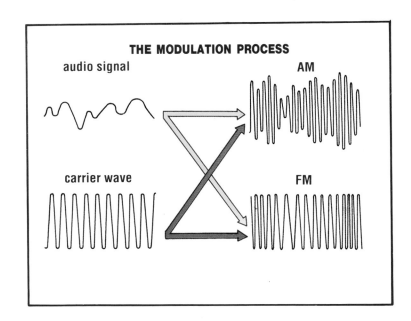

Above: The modulation process adds the sound (audio) signal to the carrier wave. There are two systems: AM (amplitude modulation), in which the strength of the carrier wave varies with the audio signal; and FM (frequency modulation), in which the frequency of the carrier wave varies with the audio signal.

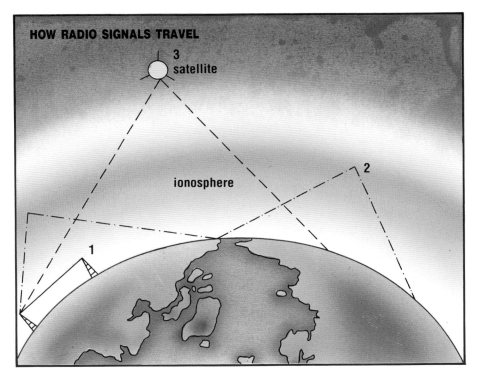

Above: How radio signals travel.
1. Some signals travel in a straight line from the transmitter to the receiver. This method can only be used for short distances. **2.** Some waves reflect off a layer of charged particles, called the ionosphere, about 50 miles high in the atmosphere. These waves, called sky waves, can travel long distances, especially if they bounce more than once. **3.** Communications satellites, circling the Earth above the atmosphere, can relay signals back to the ground.

THE TELEVISION

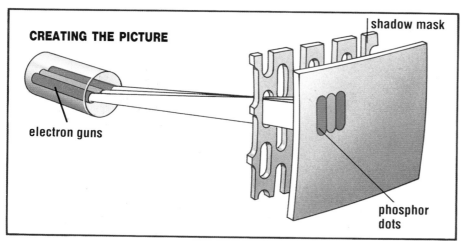

CREATING THE PICTURE

shadow mask

electron guns

phosphor dots

Left: Electromagnet coils around the electron guns direct the electron beams. The beams pass through slots in a screen called a shadow mask. This ensures that the beams fall on the phosphors of the correct color.

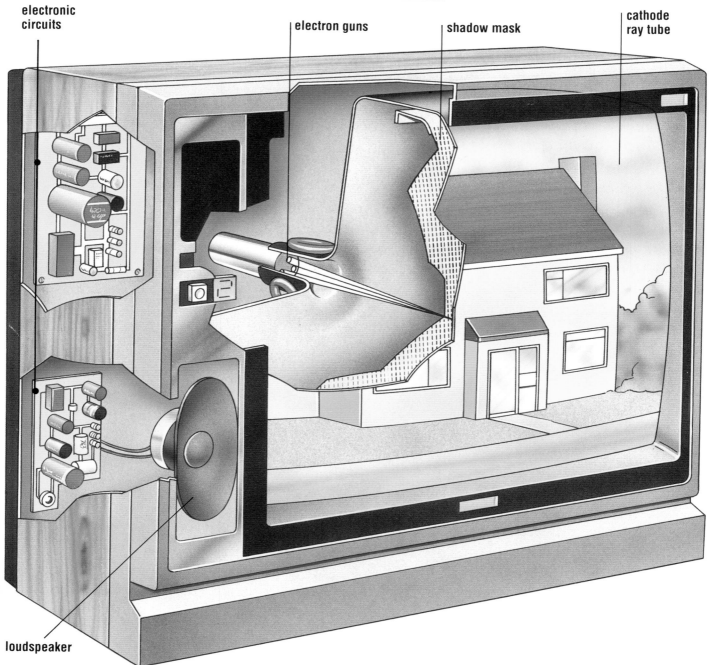

electronic circuits

electron guns

shadow mask

cathode ray tube

loudspeaker

Above: The main part of a television set is the cathode ray tube. The screen you see is one end of this tube. At the other end, electron guns shoot electrons at the screen.

Like a radio receiver, a television set has an aerial. This is designed to pick up the signals from nearby television stations. By turning the knobs or pressing the buttons on the front of the receiver, you select the signal from the station you wish to watch. Inside the receiver, the part of the signal carrying the picture is then separated from the sound signal. The sound signal is sent to the loudspeaker. The picture signal is sent to the cathode ray tube.

The television screen is one end of the cathode ray tube. It is coated inside with chemicals called phosphors. These phosphors glow when they are hit by particles of electricity called electrons. At the other end of the tube of a black and white television set is an electron gun. The gun produces electrons and shoots them toward the screen. The beam of electrons zigzags across the screen in horizontal lines. As the beam moves across the screen, the glow produced forms the picture which we see.

In a color television set, the phosphors are coated on the screen in a pattern of dots. The dots are in groups of three, one dot that glows red, one that glows blue, and one that glows green. The signal received from the aerial contains three parts corresponding to the different colors – red, blue, and green – in the picture being transmitted. These parts are fed to separate electron guns in the cathode ray tube. The electrons from the gun carrying the blue part of the picture fall on the phosphor dots that give out blue light. The electrons from the other guns fall on the red and green dots in the same way. At every spot on the screen, the three colors mix to match the colors of the original picture.

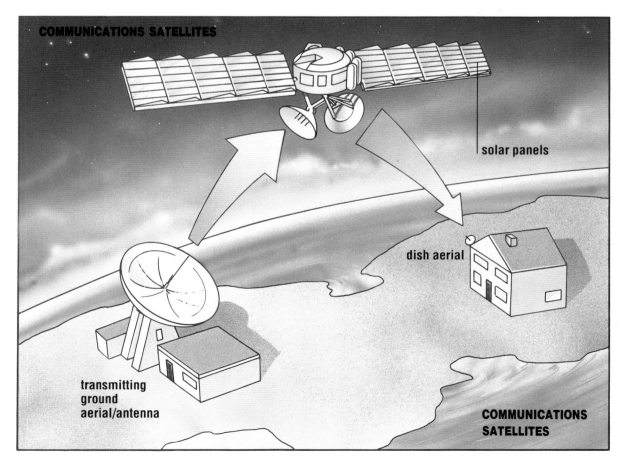

COMMUNICATIONS SATELLITES

solar panels

dish aerial

transmitting ground aerial/antenna

COMMUNICATIONS SATELLITES

Left: Communications satellites are used to transmit television signals over large distances. These satellites orbit the Earth at a height of 32,500 miles – they appear to hang stationary over one place on the Earth's surface. They pick up signals from a television station and send them back to Earth, to be picked up by small dish-shaped aerials, or antennas. The large "wings" on the satellite collect sunlight and convert it to electricity for its transmitters.

THE VIDEO RECORDER

Most video recorders store pictures on magnetic tape, although it is possible to store pictures on discs, called video discs. Video tapes are similar to the magnetic tapes used to record music and the spoken word (see pages 68–69), except that video tapes are wider than music tapes. Both types of tape are made of plastic and are covered with a fine coating of magnetic material.

If a recording is being made of a television program, the signal being received by the aerial is not sent to the television tube. Instead, the signal is sent to the recording head of the video recorder. The recording and replay heads of a video recorder are more complicated than the heads of a sound tape machine. The two heads are inside a drum which turns as the tape moves across it. The drum is tilted so that the heads produce a sloping pattern of magnetism when

they record on the tape. The pair of heads records one complete picture as a pair of sloping lines on the tape each time the drum revolves. This system enables more information to be squashed onto the tape. If this system were not used, it would take a tape 20 miles long to record a one-hour program! Sounds are recorded on a video tape in straight lines along the top and bottom of the tape. Separate audio recording and replay heads are used.

A video disc stores a picture as a pattern of small pits on the disc surface. When the disc is inserted into a special disc reader, a laser beam moves across the disc. The beam is reflected from the pits and passed on to a detector that produces an electrical signal. The signal passes to a television set connected to the disc reader and the picture is then seen on the screen.

Below: A video cassette recorder can be set to record programs over a two-week period. It can play programs in slow and fast motion, and can reverse and freeze the action. There are two popular cassette systems for home use: the Sony Betamax and the JVC VHS (Video Home System). The VHS system uses a slightly larger cassette and can hold more tape.

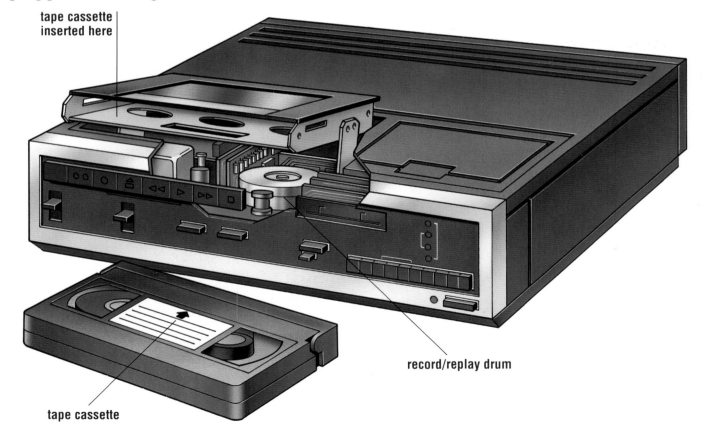

tape cassette inserted here

tape cassette

record/replay drum

THE TAPE ARRANGEMENT

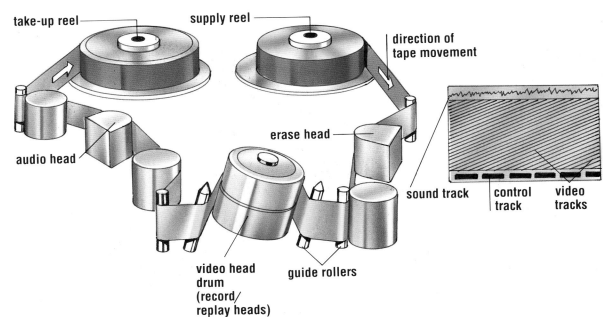

take-up reel

supply reel

direction of
tape movement

audio head

erase head

sound track

control
track

video
tracks

video head
drum
(record/
replay heads)

guide rollers

Left: Inside a video recorder, the tape is guided over the video head drum and past the audio (sound) head. The audio head records the sound track along the top of the tape. The video signal is recorded as diagonal tracks across the tape.

Below: On a video disc, pictures are stored as a pattern of tiny pits on the disc surface. A laser beam shines on the disc from underneath. The beam is reflected from the pits, and the reflected beam is converted into an electrical signal.

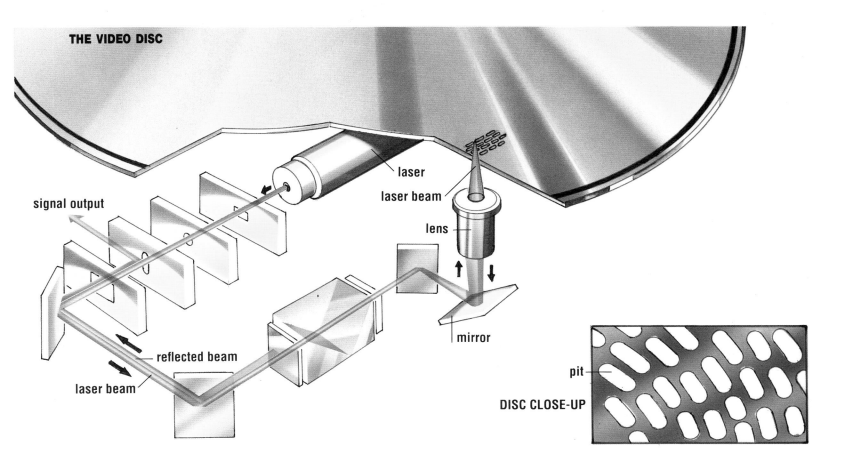

THE VIDEO DISC

signal output

laser

laser beam

lens

reflected beam

mirror

laser beam

pit

DISC CLOSE-UP

THE CAMERA

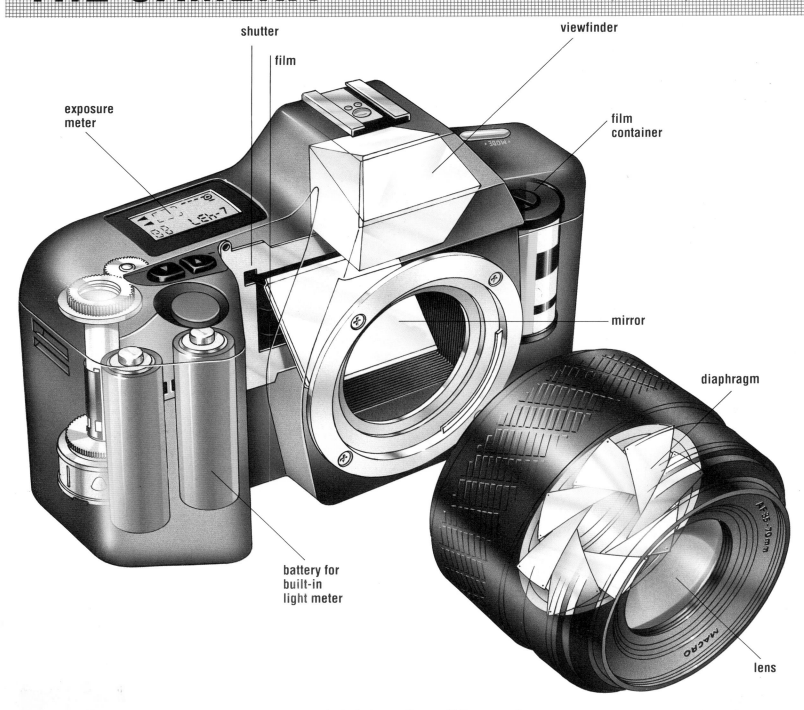

shutter

viewfinder

film

exposure meter

film container

mirror

diaphragm

battery for built-in light meter

lens

Right: Processing a black-and-white film.

1. In complete darkness, the film is placed in a developing tank.

2. A chemical called a developer is added to reveal the image on the film.

3. The image is then made permanent, or fixed, by adding a chemical called a fixer.

4. The film is washed with water to remove unwanted chemicals.

Above: A single lens reflex, or SLR, camera has a detachable lens. The diaphragm in the lens housing adjusts the size of the hole, or aperture, which lets light into the camera. The mirror directs light from the lens to the viewfinder. The shutter is just in front of the film. When a photograph is taken, the shutter opens to form a slit that moves across the film.

PROCESSING A FILM

1

2

3

4

A camera is a light-tight box with a lens at one end and a piece of film at the other end. Light enters the camera through a hole, called an aperture, in front of the lens. The lens produces an image (picture) on the film of the scene in front of the camera. A shutter, situated between the film and the lens, keeps light from reaching the film until the shutter button is pressed. Then the shutter opens, usually for only a fraction of a second. The film reacts to the light shining on it, and chemical changes take place in its light-sensitive coating. When the film is developed, the image formed on it can be seen.

The simplest camera has a single shutter speed and a fixed lens, both chosen so that on a sunny day the correct amount of light enters the camera, and the image on the film is focused (sharp). Complex cameras, designed to take perfect photographs in all kinds of lighting conditions, have shutters with a wide variety of speeds and apertures. They can also have interchangeable lenses, and built-in accessories of many kinds. Generally the main built-in accessory is an electronic exposure meter. This measures light intensity and automatically adjusts the shutter and aperture to produce a good picture.

The automatic-focus camera sends out a beam of invisible infrared light or of ultrasound – sound too high-pitched to be heard. This beam

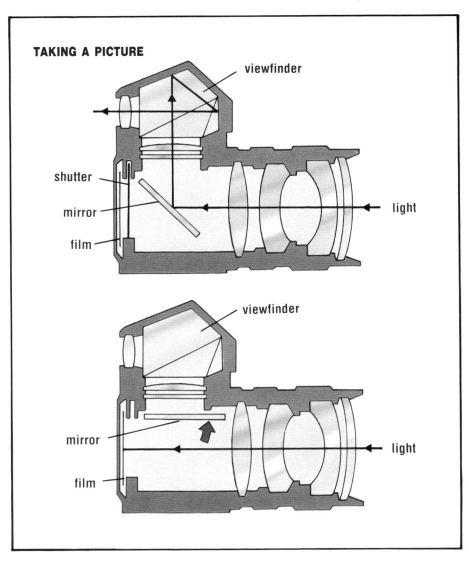

TAKING A PICTURE

viewfinder

shutter

mirror

film

light

viewfinder

mirror

film

light

bounces off the subject of the picture and returns to the camera. The time taken for the beam to return is measured, and the lens is then moved by a small motor to focus the picture and produce a clear image on the film.

Different types of film are needed for different types of picture. Fast film is suitable for dark conditions and short exposure action photography, slow film for static photographs such as portraits.

Above: The single lens reflex, or SLR, camera uses a mirror to let the user see through the lens. When the shutter is pressed, the mirror springs up to let light reach the film.

Left: Printing a film.
1. The film is placed in an enlarger and the image exposed onto photographic paper.
2. The paper is then placed in the tray and developer added.
3. The paper is washed with fixer.
4. Finally, the paper is washed with water.

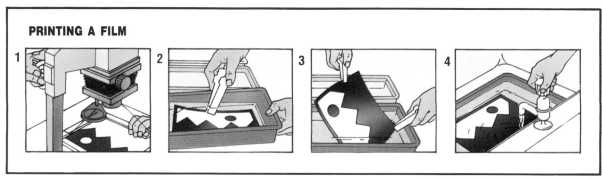

PRINTING A FILM

1   2   3   4

INDEX

Figures in **bold** refer to captions

ACKNOWLEDGMENTS

The artwork in this book was prepared by the following artists.

Hamlyn Children's Books – 15 bottom, 23 bottom

Industrial Art Studio – 18 bottom

Linden Artists – Craig Warwick 12 bottom; Tony Gibbons 24 top

The Maltings Partnership – 4–5, 6–7, 8–9, 12–13, 14–15 main, 16–17 main, 18–19 main, 20, 24–25, 26–27, 28–29, 30–31, 34–35, 36–37, 40–41, 42–43, 48–49, 60–61, 64–65, 72–73, 76–77

Russell & Russell Associates – Colin Curbishley 57, 58–59, 68–69, 70–71; Andrew McGuinness 22, 23 top, 38 top, 38–39 main, 52 bottom, 52–53 main, 62–63; David Russell 32–33, 46–47, 66, 74; Ian Thompson 10–11, 44–45 main, 50–51, 54–55

Gerald Whitcomb – 11 bottom

The Publishers would like to thank the following organizations and individuals for their kind permission to reproduce the photographs in this book.

Boeing – 15 top

EMI Classics – 67

i-Laser Sound & Vision Ltd – 53 bottom

Johnson Matthey Catalytic Systems Division – 16 top

Frank Spooner Pictures: Patrick Riviere – 21 bottom

Siemens plc – 56

Telefocus, British Telecommunications plc – 39 bottom